FROM HI-TECH TO LO-TECH

A WOODWORKER'S JOURNEY

NORMAN PIROLLO

Copyright © 2015 Norman Pirollo

All rights reserved. No portion of this book may be used without sole permission of the copyright holder except in use of a review.

Published by New Art Press

The publisher and authors have attempted to be as accurate as possible in the creation of this book. The content, including but not limited to: statistics, screenshots, availability of products, etc., are as accurate as possible, as of publication date. Due to the rapidly changing nature of the Internet, some statistics, terms of service, etc., may have changed. While all attempts have been made to verify the information provided in this publication, neither the authors nor the publisher assume any responsibility for errors, omissions, or contrary interpretations of the subject matter herein. The views expressed are those of the authors alone and should not be taken as expert instruction or commands. The reader is responsible for his or her own actions.

Some of the links (excluding any and all links to Amazon.com) in this eBook may be 'affiliate links'. This means if you click on the link and purchase the item, we may receive an affiliate commission. Please understand that we only recommend products or services we use personally and believe will add value to our readers. We are disclosing this in accordance with the Federal Trade Commission's 16 CFR, Part 255: 'Guides Concerning the Use of Endorsements and Testimonials'.

Typeset in Cambria with permission from Microsoft.

ISBN-13: 978-0973071054
ISBN-10: 0973071052

Cover image attribution: WoodSkills: Norman Pirollo (Own work)

Page 24 image (Altair 8800) attribution: By Swtpc6800 en: User: Swtpc6800 Michael Holley (Own work) [Public domain], via Wikimedia Commons

Page 170 image attribution: Fine Woodworking Magazine "4 Bench Jigs for Handplanes" Fine Woodworking Magazine Issue No. 202

From Hi-Tech to Lo-Tech

A Woodworker's Journey

Norman Pirollo

Contents

Introduction i
   The Early Years 3
   The Formative Years 9
   A Career 27
   Creative Discovery 55
   Learning Curve 65
   Layoff Shock 71
   A First Business 77
   A Return To School 85
   A Summer Project 91
   A New Phase 97
   A New Millennium 103
   A Dilemma 113
   A New Direction 119
   The Business Of Woodworking 127

Hand Tool Redux	141
New Work Methods	153
A Fascination With Cabinets	161
Three Strikes	175
WoodSkills	189
Furniture Design + Build	197
Conclusion	219
About The Author	220

Introduction

"We do not remember days, we remember moments"

Cesare Pavese

I WROTE THIS BOOK to share my creative journey from childhood through adulthood. Perseverance, fate, and critical decisions all combined to map out the direction I followed in life. Looking back at my early youth, it can be seen that creativity was always my strong point. As the journey progressed, creative outlets were often sought in life. Woodworking ultimately became my creative outlet. Many obstacles were faced throughout the journey and financial support was often at the forefront. I enjoy where I am today in life, having accumulated considerable experience and expertise at several woodworking businesses. Much is also owed to my former hi-tech career, which provided me fulfillment for a number of years.

There were many false starts in transitioning from full-time employment to being self-employed. The opportunity to work at something I truly enjoy has ultimately brought solace and independence to my life. I never look back at missed opportunities. Gratitude is also owed to a supportive family, friends and colleagues who inspired my journey. It is important to have a spouse or partner that supports your journey. It is also important to view any setbacks as valuable experience in your own journey. The time and effort invested in following your own dream will be well worth it.

Norman Pirollo

The Early Years

"Life isn't a matter of milestones, but of moments"

Rose Kennedy

MY FAMILY HERITAGE HAS always been technical in nature. My father often described how his family operated an established fireworks company in his native country. Putting on fireworks was a large part of festivals and events in the early part of the 20th century. There was fierce competition among a few fireworks firms and ingenuity always won out. The ingenuity that took the form of new and exciting fireworks demonstrations drove my family. My father's family livelihood depended on putting on flawless, exciting fireworks shows. It is this business that spurred a technical superiority race that brought out the ingenuity in my ancestral family. My grandfather was a watchmaker and I can only imagine the fine, detail work involved. His patience and precision of working with miniature parts hopefully rubbed off on me.

Listening to these family tales made me proud. There were many stories about having to create unique tools and furniture. Even as a young boy, these stories began to be an inspiration to me. At this early age, I watched as my father attempted his own repairs on broken household items. He had created a small shop area for himself with a workbench and a good assortment of tools. The tools had been accumulated over a period of decades. My father had at different points in his life worked as a welder, shoe maker, and shop foreman.

It is obvious that the trades were a focal point of my upbringing. Although my father progressed to white collar work later in life, he maintained a workshop with tools and small machines to craft small parts and repair broken appliances. As a young boy, I saw the amount of time my father spent tinkering with small motors and repairing anything mechanical that was broken. He had the attitude that everything could be repaired; it was not necessary to replace an object simply because it was broken. This pervasive attitude wore off on me and motivated me to tinker with small motors and anything mechanical.

It was from the age of ten to twelve that my interest in electrical and mechanical machines began in earnest. At this age, I was already a copious reader and was beginning to borrow science books from the municipal library. A particularly keen interest was developing in the early inventors of radio technology and electronics. Marconi and Tesla come to mind as the subject matter I was delving in at this age.

Long before the Internet age, the only method to learn about a subject was through books. In my younger years, there was not a local library in my area, so I often made the trek to a large municipal library and borrowed a series of books. The books would be read from cover to cover and I often naively tried to reproduce some of the experiments. Early radio technology fascinated me and small passive receivers using "cats' whisker" technology were prominent in my experiments. The development of radio by Guglielmo Marconi was followed and I attempted to replicate some of the early devices. Often, these experiments worked, encouraging me to try more complex experiments.

My family was fairly large with many siblings, three brothers, and three sisters. The age difference shared with my siblings precluded me from sharing my interests with my brothers. Although we each developed shared interests over the years, the age differential in my early to teen years isolated me in my interests. As with many large families, I must admit feeling a little different than most young boys of my age group. Although I had a circle of friends, my interests lay in science and not sports. Of course, time was spent with other boys my age, but my growing interest in science soon took over.

Once a good understanding was had of how the science functioned, I found myself dreaming of grandiose experiments. At the age of twelve, components were often gathered for many of these experiments in the hope of assembling a radio receiver, a motor or a transmitter. I also had other interests in this period. My older stepbrother would bring copies home of Popular Science and Popular Mechanics. At the age of eleven or twelve, I would read these magazines and find the advertisements to be seducing. There were considerable ads about science experiments you could make yourself by purchasing plans, and some included the necessary components. Many of the ads also focused on stamp collecting. Offers to send you a small starter kit of stamps at a very reasonable price were inviting. One particular mail order offer drew me in and launched my stamp-collecting hobby. Part of the sales pitch was the encouragement to sell stamps to friends. Stamps would be purchased from a company at wholesale prices where my friends were then be set up as stamp collectors. I then became the stamp supplier or middleman. This was a fun experience for a few months, but I kept returning to science as my passion!

The mid to late 1960s was an exciting time in the world of science and technological innovation. The space program was peaking and a lunar landing was to be the high point of the decade. Scientific developments abounded. Popular in this era were kits where you would build your own electronic devices. Heathkit was a very popular platform for kit building of radio receivers, transmitters, and amplifiers. I slowly began to lust after many of the kits in the Heathkit catalog. The prices, although they were kits, were fairly expensive. There were different kits at different price points. These products were either sold through mail order or locally at electronic hobby stores. The alternative was to study how early devices were put together and instead make my own. Sourcing the components was accomplished by tearing down old radios. I often visited what we would call **junk stores** in the day. They had a very large assortment of early radios complete with mechanical tuners, transformers, and all the necessary small electronic components. These junk stores provided endless entertainment. It was exciting for me to see how many of the early radios and electronic devices were assembled.

By walking down the aisles, the evolution of radio and electronic technology could be witnessed before my very eyes. Most of the electronics were taken apart, exposing circuit boards and sheet metal assemblies. Attempts have been made at understanding why I developed such a fascination with mechanical and electronic objects at such an early age. Was it because of my innate curiosity? Was it the maker in me beginning to blossom? Was it a need to satisfy a craving for understanding science? Or was it all of the above.

Magazines such as Popular Science and Popular Mechanics held me in awe. Technological innovation and developments were many; color photos made it all real. Many of the images were only illustrations but at a young age they might as well be real. I recall feeling overwhelmed in keeping up with so many advancements. Reading and re-reading science articles to attempt to understand the technical jargon had become a welcome challenge. The technical terms and descriptions I began to learn excited me and with it came a new vocabulary.

The advancements in missile technology in this period could be recalled. Terms such as ABM (anti-ballistic missile) and MAD (mutually assured destruction) were being tossed around where few people knew the meaning. I took it upon myself to learn what this new missile technology was and enjoyed talking about it with friends.

Looking back, standing up in class at the age of twelve with an understanding of these terms was remarkable. It was in my early teen years that a fascination for all things mechanical and electrical developed. At this young age, many of the devices we took for granted were instead mysteries to me. The exploratory path into how things worked led me to discover mechanical and electrical principles. The trial and error process of making and testing devices made the journey even more exciting.

I was fortunate to have a father that had a good grasp of tools and how to use them. I watched how he would use his tools and mimicked many of the steps involved. We built things together. This was an era where many fathers tinkered with small engines and motors. The do it yourself philosophy was widespread. Mechanical and electronic kits were available through many mail order supply houses.

I was also close to my older stepbrother, Eugene. His passion was cars, where he would drive various used cars home on several occasions. He loved tinkering with engines and I would watch and try to understand. Along with several manuals, he had a sizeable collection of car and engine parts. On several occasions, I took the liberty to flip through the manuals. Questions were asked, he would explain. Eugene was much older, but I was old enough to participate with him in his pastime. He would take me everywhere in his late model sports car, where talk was often about cars and mechanics. Since this time, I have been fascinated with auto mechanics and engines and owe this to him. Later in the 1968-69 period, I often accompanied him when building his new house. This was a home he completely designed and built on his own. This experience would be another introduction to tools and working with wood in my journey!

Often in this era, the only means of owning something mechanical or electronic was by building it yourself. Every teenager owned a bicycle in my youth, much like today. Bicycle technology was also evolving at a rapid pace. Three-speed bikes became five-speed bikes and then evolved into ten-speed bikes. Derailleur technology was fairly new and exciting at the time. This new cycle technology was fully embraced and I began to build myself a bicycle. It had to be a long-fork model, popular at the time. We typically used parts from other derelict bicycles to create the fork extensions. The five-speed derailleur was retrofitted to the rear wheels since this type of bicycle could not be purchased. A derailleur is the gear mechanism that enables different gear ratios to be selected from the main pedal gear to the rear wheel.

Much ingenuity went into the design of these bicycles. Stability was another story, however, and weight distribution of the bike was an issue on more than one occasion. The experience of this do it yourself bike building period made me appreciate my first store-bought bicycle; a fancy racing model with two sets of derailleurs. My bicycle building phase lasted four years from the age of twelve to age sixteen. The common theme in all this is the creativity involved in building and making something from parts. Used bicycle parts could be had from bike stores and it was then simply an exercise in ingenuity to put together a bicycle that worked.

Aside from the technical and scientific side of my early years, I had a normal life of participating in some sports while studying at school. Ice hockey was a large part of the youth culture at the time and still is. My family home was located across from an outdoor ice hockey rink that was frozen over in winter and maintained by the city. To be able to play ice hockey, I taught myself how to skate. My friends and I would lace up our skates after school and head over to the ice rink. Often, the ice rink would need to be cleared of snow, and shovels were always around to be able to perform this task. The rink was well lit so we could play until late in the evening. Ice hockey was the preferred winter sport in my neighborhood. There were always enough friends around to set up a hockey game. Friendships and rivalries were created through hockey, all part of my youth.

Around the age of eleven, two individuals approached me from a large daily newspaper in the city. They were seeking a newspaper delivery boy for the area and I recall agreeing to this right on the spot. The arrangement was that there would be a stack of newspapers delivered to my home each day with a list of subscribers and their addresses. A small amount was paid to me per subscriber and the gratuities could be kept. At the time, this was very exciting and I felt like a young businessman. My parents weren't very thrilled since this would involve walking many streets on my own. Nevertheless, this gig lasted for a year or so and the tips were good. This might have been my introduction to business at a very young age. Some spending money of my own was earned to be able to buy whatever pleased me.

In 1968, at the age of twelve, a summer position to sell magazine subscriptions was presented to me. The hiring company would drive a few of us to different parts of the city where we would go door to door selling magazine subscription packages. There would be greater compensation when more magazines were bundled together. The tips were great and more disposable money was available to finance my scientific experiments and purchases.

The Formative Years

"In youth we learn; in age we understand"

Marie von Ebner-Eschenbach

MY EARLY TEEN YEARS brought many challenges and experiences to my life. As a fairly shy young teenager, large groups were shunned; instead time was spent with a small circle of good friends. Age thirteen was a seminal year in my youth. Primary school years had ended and secondary school was beginning. The secondary school assigned to me was miles away and this involved taking city buses to get to and from school. Around this time, new friendships were begun with colleagues I had met in my classes.

The secondary school system was a revelation. In primary school, we were always seated in the same classroom, where different teachers would rotate through and teach different subjects throughout the day. In secondary school, the students instead had to change classrooms. We were provided a curriculum of classes to take with specific classroom numbers. Each class had a different teacher pertaining to the subject being taught. There was a strict dress code in the first and second years of secondary school. A shirt, tie, and jacket were mandatory. This is mentioned because the dress code soon disappeared. This was the 1969-70 era and many rules were being relaxed.

By 1971, the students at the secondary school could wear anything they pleased as long as the clothes were not provocative. In this era, many societal rules and norms were being relaxed along with dress codes. People tended to dress more informally. An atmosphere of rebellion was in the air. Soon, jeans were commonplace in the school environment. Hair length for males was no longer short, longer hair was the norm. I recall that people began to look sloppily dressed, but it was a liberating time.

The author, Norman Pirollo, at the age of 14 in 1970

It was also a confusing time. How to dress was often on the mind. As time went on, the proper school uniform was replaced with jeans and a jean jacket. As a young adolescent, I was extremely self-conscious of how to dress as it was important to fit in with other students. An informal dress code of jeans was adopted. Ironically, we dressed the same anyway, simply wearing a trendier set of clothes instead of a uniform. My interest in school became stronger at age thirteen but began to wane a little afterwards. There were many distractions I recall. Students tended to join small groups of fellow students where peer pressure was strong.

If you were part of a group of students, you were expected to participate in the activities of the group. Fortunately, I soon realized that it was best to be part of a studious group. The studious students typically excelled in their grades, attended all classes, and sat at the front of the class. I became friends with a small group of teens that had studies as a priority.

Although tending to dress as a rebel, this group of teens kept me from being influenced by other groups. I once again enjoyed studying and thrived in the competitive nature of the group. It was almost essential to maintain high grades to be part of this circle of friends. This fostered a healthy rivalry between us. To this day, I am thankful for being part of this group as it was too easy to succumb to the enticements of other teen groups. We studied together, helped each other out on assignments, and exchanged views. Allegiance was maintained to this group of students for most of my secondary years and it served me well.

My father had retired during this period and started a small home-based business. He found a niche in sharpening cutlery, scissors and anything with an edge on it. He then invested in a couple of tool grinders and fashioned tool rests to hold the various tools and cutlery that needed sharpening. Until this time, my father held a white-collar business position in real estate. One day, he decided to walk away from it all and instead follow his passion of working with small tools, repairing broken equipment and tinkering in his shop.

I don't recall exactly how he stumbled on to the sharpening of tools. He was soon successful at sharpening and word traveled in the neighborhood that my father provided a sharpening service. He enjoyed the initial success, as it brought him many different tools with cutting edges. He was able to gain experience sharpening each of these tool types as he progressed from sharpening knives to scissors and then saw blades. The clientele began to come from near and far once word got around. His next step was to set up a proper home-based business. There was a zoning issue that he overcame and he was able to place signage outside as advertising for the business.

My father soon saw the business potential of having an ice rink across the street and this motivated him to acquire ice skate sharpening equipment. Soon he mastered the sharpening of ice skates. Throughout the winter, ice skate sharpening business was regular. The prices he charged were very reasonable since his overhead was fairly low except for the equipment, grinding wheels and sanding belts.

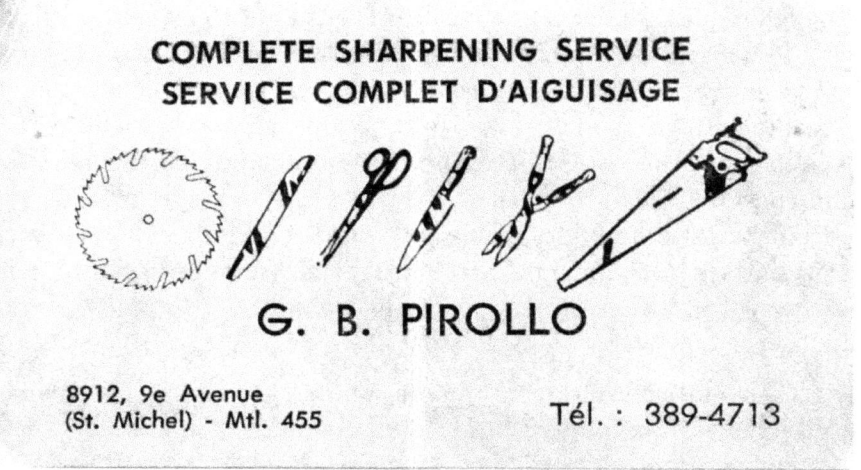

First business card of my fathers' sharpening business (1971)

I watched in amazement as the clientele grew. Clients were so satisfied with his work that they would gratuitously tip him. There was a gleam in his eye each time he mentioned how happy a customer was and the large tip they left. Repeat business was regular; clients would drop off cutlery or tools to be sharpened and pick them up two days later. Business was great and growing. To this day, I am amazed how my father stumbled on to this lucrative business niche. He would often begin work very early in the morning to keep his free time for later. I would help my father out as often as possible after school. This gave me an education in how to use tools.

It was around this time that my father noticed my developing shyness. As a young fourteen year old teenager, I was coping with it, but my father realized that being shy would be a career impediment. He had an idea to help me overcome my shyness. His business was for the most part limited to the neighborhood.

He had wanted to expand but was not sure how. The idea was to have me travel throughout the city, knock on business doors with a business card and ask for sharpening business. We came to a financial arrangement where I would receive a very good percentage of any work brought to him.

We worked on a plan where I would do certain routes each week. Sharpening work was picked up after school, delivered to my father and returned the next day. More work was then picked up from other clients on the route. The routes were all easily accessible by transit or if not too far, by bicycle. During the day, I attended school and would begin collecting work after school and weekends. I recall the awkwardness of entering businesses and introducing myself the first few times. Striking up conversations was difficult. Perhaps the clients sympathized with me, but I began to collect sharpening work.

My shyness was slowly overcome as I became more comfortable talking to people, who were for the most part strangers. This part-time work was a success for both my father and I, and we got along very well. My father was often impressed with the amount of sharpening work I would bring back, although there were slow periods. This part-time employment continued for approximately three years from the age of fourteen to seventeen. In this time, I had begun to accumulate a sizeable amount of spending money. This money was used to purchase much of my own clothing, shoes, school books and bicycles. The largest benefit was the success in overcoming my shyness. Although retaining some shyness; my fear of conversation with complete strangers had largely been overcome.

My father and I had created a bond, which carried us into the next years. I often look back at this accomplishment and how we both worked at building a business. This was my first foray into business and it was a successful one. I have very fond memories of this period of my life and partnering with my father.

My father, John Pirollo, in his younger years in Canada (1935)

The next period of my teen years included summer job employment and continued academic studies at secondary school. My school studies included the standard courses taught as part of the curriculum.

A few of these courses were easier than others and considerable time was spent studying to maintain a good grade average. My circle of friends was fairly small in this period; recalling only two to three good friends. These particular friends were an influence on me in a positive way. They were intelligent and studious and I looked up to them as they looked up to me. The middle years of secondary school were not terribly exciting with very little guidance until this point. The path to take after completing secondary school had not yet determined. The importance of going to university was drilled into me and this kept me constantly motivated in attaining good grades. We were told how important high grades were, as this determined which students would be accepted or rejected from a university.

My hobbies during this time ranged from building scientific projects found in magazine articles to short wave radio listening. I recall purchasing at least two radio receivers that had the capability of receiving shortwave bands. This was fascinating to me; to be able to hear radio broadcasts from around the world. Sitting on the front steps of my home, countless hours were spent fine-tuning the radio receiver to listen to broadcasts in different foreign languages.

Surplus stores were also visited very often along with the so-called "junk" stores. Older technology items were purchased and taken apart in the hope of salvaging components that could be useful in a project. Tearing apart old devices and electronics gave me the understanding of the involvement of their assembly. Intricate soldering that was probably performed on assembly lines, since computerized soldering did not exist at the time. It was intriguing to see how precisely the cables and wires were routed to keep from interfering with each other. How certain high voltage wires were bundled together and kept separate from low voltage wires.

I often challenged myself by taking apart electronics and putting them back together. The exciting moment was when my fingers were crossed and the unit plugged into a wall socket. Many of these early electronic devices and receivers were powered with tube technology. It was often simply a burnt tube that kept the radio receiver or device from operating.

Tubes were still commonplace in electronics in the late 1960s and very early 1970s. Tube testers could be found in local drugstores. A burnt tube replacement would often originate from the selection of tubes accumulated from tearing apart other electronic devices. The process of tearing apart and re-assembling electronics would give me a better understanding of how these devices functioned. Discrete electronics and active tubes combined with mechanical condensers came together to create an operating receiver or transmitter. After a few tear downs, a good understanding of older electronic devices was developed.

This was also an indeterminate time for me; a time where I was too young to legally work at a summer job. For a period of one or two years, I instead helped my father at his business and continued to gather sharpening work for him. We worked together in developing techniques for sharpening new tools such as lawnmower blades. The constant exposure to tools and the creation of specialized tools would be of great benefit to me later in life.

By this time, my sharpening routes had been mastered and an established clientele had developed. Many of the clients would call for pick up and a schedule would then be set up. In the process, many facets of business were learned from how to acquire business, manage business and handle money. These were valuable traits that I have applied to business later in life, having started four of my own businesses. All this kept me so busy my shyness was completely forgotten!

The secondary school years were also very developmental to me. I began the period as a naive young adolescent and was soon introduced to the many foibles of man. This period was the very early 1970s and rapid change was everywhere. Tradition was being shunned at every turn. Religion used to be a large part of our lives, now it was hardly ever discussed among my peers. Interestingly enough, religion was still taught at the secondary school level, but at more of a philosophical level. The youth at the time was becoming increasingly rebellious. The rebellion was in the form of clothing worn, extracurricular activities and risky behavior. Somehow I survived these influences and continued on with a good grade average.

All the while, the goal of being accepted to a university was on my mind. Towards the latter years of secondary school, it became considerably more critical to have an academic plan in place. In the last year of high school, a few courses were electives, based on the program followed after secondary school. We had to decide on an academic choice for post-secondary education. My first exposure to computers was on a class visit to a mainframe center of a large company. The large mainframes consisted of typical computers of the era complete with spinning tapes and flashing lights.

The technology mesmerized me, but this was to be my only exposure to computers for a few years. I had always had a deep interest in electronics and anything electric. My guidance counselor in 1972 praised the virtues of a new three year electro technology program at the college level. The choice was then between a three year vocational type program and a two year pre-university program. Soon, a decision would need to be made!

A close friend at the time convinced me of the opportunities an electronics diploma would bring. As a testament to his belief, Carmelo Lattuca enrolled in the program. I soon followed and in doing so hoped to erase any doubts in my mind as to which post-secondary program to follow. We were also told that we could continue on to university and pursue an engineering degree after graduating from the three year electrotechnology program. Although this would be a very demanding three years, I ultimately enrolled in this new electro-technology program. If employment could not be found after graduating, pursuing a university degree was always an option.

Throughout my secondary school years, I had become a voracious reader of anything technical and made a point to understand how things worked. Devices would be torn apart and put back together as well as reading about the devices to understand their functionality. The common thread of my adolescent and teen years was the education gained from hands-on use of tools, and the curiosity channeled into scientific projects and experiments. This lay the groundwork for the next phase of my life.

A few months after graduating from secondary school in early 1973, I began to attend college. The new electro-technology program promised many opportunities upon graduation. The program was new and exciting to me. Many of the scientific experiments and radio projects worked on as a youth were often trial and error. Aside from reading about electronics and radio technology, I had no academic background in these subjects. The first year of the electro technology program consisted of the basics with which to understand electronics.

Courses such as Calculus, Physics, A/C Electronics and D/C Electronics, Resistance, Capacitance, Voltage, Current, and Drafting were the initial courses. Early experiments performed while in my teens helped me to understand various electric and electronic formulas. I finally had a good grasp of how electronic devices worked and were put together!

The program consisted of both theory and practical application of algorithms and formulas. The laboratories in the college were fairly well equipped to be able to test all kinds of motor formulas. We had oscilloscopes and test instruments available to perform precise scientific analysis of input and output. The practical application of what we learned was invaluable in the learning process. Reading about and understanding theories only went so far in learning, where actually creating and testing circuitry reinforced it all.

THE FORMATIVE YEARS

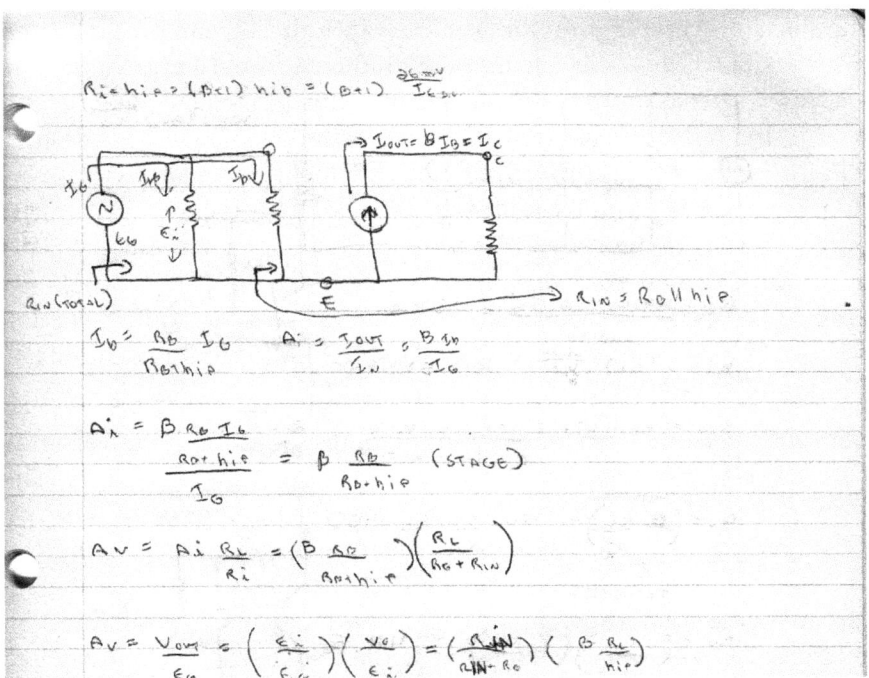

Notes from my first year in the Electro technology Program (1973)

The students I associated with were fairly studious and we helped each other in comprehending the various theories. My close friend Carmelo and I would share in the understanding of the lectures. As part of each lab assignment, we either chose a lab partner or were assigned one. In selecting a lab partner, usually a fellow student I had good experience from a previous lab exercise was chosen. It became critical to choose someone who had a good grasp of the theories since this would also help me to understand the subject.

We bread-boarded various circuits to be able to test resistance, voltage, impedance, current draw, etc. The circuits had pre-defined electronic components and the output readings were specific. This helped us to compare notes where we could determine if we were performing the lab exercise correctly. We had plenty of hands-on laboratory exercises in the form of practical applications of circuits.

The electro-technology diploma path was a three-year program and each year of studies was considerably different from the previous. The first year focused on prerequisite mathematics, calculus, algebra, and physics. Introductory electronics was also taught as part of the first year. The second year introduced more advanced electronics formulas and algorithms into the program. Motor technology, radio communications, tube and transistor technology were taught. This curriculum formed the core of a well-rounded electro technologist career. The third year consisted of a few core courses and a selection of electives. A student could either follow the radio communications or a computer studies path.

Even with my keen interest in radio communications, I viewed it as yesterday's technology. The computer field was growing quickly. The development of computers and integrated circuits that were the core of computers completely fascinated me. Integrated circuit technology was approximately ten years old by the early 1970s. The number of discrete components such as transistors, which could be mounted on an IC chip, was doubling each year. By the mid-1970s, technology had advanced to where microprocessors, also known as "computers on a chip", were being manufactured.

The three-year college program was begun in the fall of 1973 at the age of seventeen and was completed in the spring of 1976 at the age of nineteen. As an introduction to computers, we were taught a programming language in the first year. The language was the ubiquitous COBOL. Learning to program with COBOL involved entering a program on punched cards and submitting it to a mainframe computer to be compiled. A day or so later we picked up the results. More often than not we had entered incorrect code and this involved repeating the cycle of submitting and waiting for results. The process was tedious and frustrating and turned many students away from computer technology. Little did we know that this punched card technology was on its last legs and would soon be replaced with computer monitors and keyboards. Computer monitors and keyboards would revolutionize the computer world. Results could be acquired instantly and compiles performed in minutes!

THE FORMATIVE YEARS   21

I chose to focus on computer studies in the last year of the electro-technology program, selecting all computer technology related electives. We learned about discrete chips such as amplifiers, logic chips such as AND gates, OR gates, and Flip Flops. Laboratory exercises consisted of bread-boarding a few of these Integrated Circuit **IC** chips to create a circuit which toggled a flip-flop or lit an LED.

Circuit board assembled while in Electro Technology Program (1975)

Computers operated on BOOLEAN logic (1's and 0's) and we had to learn how to assemble strings of Boolean numbers and to convert these strings into Octal or Decimal. The excitement of learning about this exciting new computer technology, essentially in its infancy, was overwhelming.

Advancements were being announced on a weekly basis. Microcomputer chips were being assembled into a new class of computers called microcomputers. I recall being of the opinion that every other technology was in the dark ages compared to this new microcomputer technology.

The final or third year of the program involved completing a fairly large project in each of the semesters. The first project was to assemble a slew of IC gates, flip-flops and drivers to emulate a very primitive Boolean calculator or very basic computer. The design of the circuit was as important as actually making it. Weeks were spent designing a fairly complex circuit with many IC's. The Boolean logic behind this circuit was very complex. Different circuit paths were followed depending on which gates or flip-flops were toggled. The design worked very well on paper. Next, all the components were assembled on a breadboard. Interestingly enough, the design did work in real life. This success instilled great confidence in me as I continued to immerse myself in computer technology.

There were two upstart magazines in this era that catered specifically to microcomputers and related technology. Subscribing to both magazines, every attempt was made to understand the articles. Microcomputer kit offerings with toggle switches and blinking lights shown in magazine advertising and articles were mesmerizing. The magazines, **Byte** and **Interface Age**, had become fairly popular and gained a large, loyal following. To this day, a few of the more popular issues are part of my current collection of magazines and books. Two popular kit offerings at the time were the **IMSAI 8080** and the Altair 8800 microcomputers. Prices for these kits were expensive as microchip technology was fairly recent and the family of chips necessary to build these microcomputers was not yet mainstream. Lusting after these microcomputer kits, I would one day buy one and build my own microcomputer.

Byte Magazine cover from January 1977, featuring the Altair 8800 (from my collection)

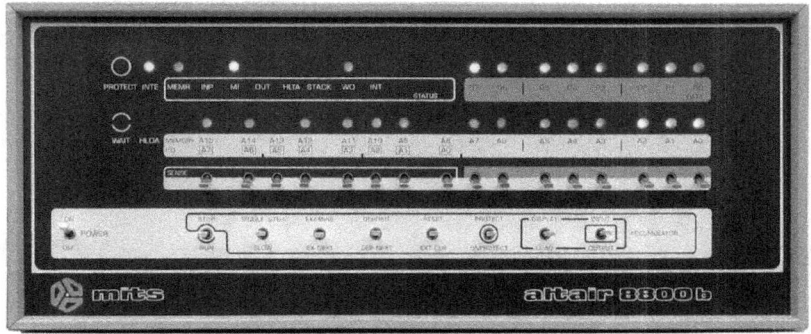

Altair 8800 Microcomputer with toggle switches and lamps (1976)

Part of the final year of the computer technology curriculum was to work on actual computers. We had a few commercial minicomputers to work with and were provided with programs to key in and then view results. Although it sounds primitive today, computers of the day were programmed through toggle switches. After having briefly worked with punched card technology, computer monitors and keyboards were a godsend. Computers were now more appealing to work with!

After completing the first semester of my final year at college, I could not wait to begin the second semester. The second semester brought an intensive workload of studies with it. The courses focused mainly on computers and IC amplification. Each student had a project to complete where a selection of projects was available. The decision was made to design and build a computer monitor. The project details were provided as well as some of the circuitry. Parts would need to be assembled with the parts to build a functioning computer monitor with keyboard. Unlike today, this technology was relatively new and primitive at the time. Scan lines would often be seen across the monitor screen if the circuitry was incorrectly set up.

The project was successfully completed and a great deal was learned from the process. I graduated from the three year electro-technology program with excellent grades. In the final weeks of the semester, various local companies attended the school to begin an employee hiring selection process.

Each student met with a representative from a company and interviews were performed. It was only in the last few days of the semester that the companies announced which students they would like to work for them. An appealing early offer of employment was presented to me, but I held out to determine if any better offers came in. This particular offer involved working for a large computer corporation headquartered in the US. My role would be as a local technician to work on their computers at client sites.

Learning to program would also be a necessary part of my training. At the time, it was rewarding to be able to work in a field I truly enjoyed. Money was secondary to me at this stage of my life. After graduating in May of 1976 at the age of nineteen, my employment began at this first company **MAI** that had interviewed me.

A Career

"Try to learn something about everything and everything about something"

Thomas Huxley

THE FIRST YEAR AT MY NEW CAREER would be an eye-opener. I was immediately thrust into the world of commercial minicomputers. Minicomputers had by now been available for a few years and were much smaller and less expensive than their predecessor, the mainframe. This allowed many small to medium sized businesses to have their own in-house computers. Previously, a small company would have to lease time on a mainframe to manage their employee records, inventory, and sales. With the advent of this new class of minicomputers, prices had become affordable enough for a small company to purchase or lease their own computer system.

A service agreement was usually bundled in with each sale of these minicomputer systems. Minicomputer systems would periodically fail as mechanical disk storage drives were part of every system. Fans would stop working, disk heads would crash and circuitry would act up or stop functioning. Although the reliability of these systems was good, each small company with a computer system had to protect themselves from computer failure.

So much business continuity was riding on these computer systems that uptime became important to these small to medium sized companies. This is where my role as computer technician entered. My job was to ensure that a specific set of clients were catered to. It was necessary for me to travel to client sites and periodically run diagnostics to detect an imminent failure. My role also involved performing maintenance on the systems. Upon a computer failure, I would be sent to the client site to run diagnostics in an attempt to isolate a faulty component. These clients had access to a hotline to have me dispatched to their site within a few hours. There would be a few of us in the Technical Department of the computer company **MAI** and we covered for each other from time to time. If, for example, one of us was busy at another client site for longer than expected. After joining this first company **MAI**, I was to be sent away on training for a period of seven weeks. The training was located at their Canadian training headquarters and consisted of a combination of hardware and software courses. Programming their computers to effectively run diagnostics and learning how to repair the hardware was taught in the training.

In the weeks leading up to training, I tagged along with an experienced MAI technician, Gerry Valente. My role was to watch, learn and be of any assistance. The weeks leading up to my training were beneficial, and the time was found to be productive. Gerry was instrumental at instilling a professional work ethic and customer communication skills in me. Soon, I would become familiar enough with the computers to better grasp information taught in the upcoming training. The freedom this particular type of work brought with it was also appreciated. Alternative employment would likely have been in a laboratory setting as a technologist or test technician. In this new position, it was necessary to drive to client sites, develop my social skills and enjoy freedom between dispatches or "service calls". At the young age of nineteen, life could not get better! At the formal **MAI** company training, my immersion into programming the software and hardware of these computer systems had begun.

Intent on being successful at this position, every minute of my training was valued. Questions were asked and programming code was written to be able to control the minicomputers. The computer language of choice of MAI computers was **BASIC**, a fairly straightforward English-like interpreter software language. The BASIC language was only a few years old at this time and very popular, as it was not too difficult to write the code. We were given exercises where we wrote increasingly complex programs to control the computer system. As part of the training, we were also taught to diagnose common problems experienced with these minicomputers. There was a sense of camaraderie with the other students in the training group and we got along well.

The seven-week period went by very quickly and daily classroom sessions instilled a vast amount of knowledge in us. At the formal graduation at the end of the training, we were handed a diploma. To better understand the subject material, I recall studying on the weekends. At the time, it was understood that this training was invaluable with only one good attempt at taking it. Upon my return from training, a used car was purchased and my role began as a computer technician. I was now performing the job on my own and without assistance, although help was available to me at any time. The company maintained second level support engineers to assist technicians that were stuck on difficult problems. The more difficult problems were intermittent and difficult to diagnose as they only occurred under certain circumstances.

As time went on, the job was quickly mastered and I became more at ease with it. Throughout the upcoming months, several difficult problems were encountered. These problems were typically intermittent problems where it was necessary to diagnose and replace many components and circuit boards to arrive at a solution. Often the problem was mechanical in nature. The storage medium of choice of this era was the magnetic disk drive. Ceramic heads would float above rotating disks. These heads would read and write information onto disk tracks. Often, dirty heads would touch a disk surface and eventually cause a "head crash".

```
10 PRINT @ ("SF", @(30,3), "ENTRIES"
20 DIM Z$(75,"*")
25 PRINT @(3,5), Z$
30 PRINT @(5,7), "ITEM #", @(17,7), "DESCR.", @(30,7), "QUANT",
   @(42,7), "PRICE PER *", @(60,7), "TOTAL $"
34 LET K=9
36 LET K= K+1
40 INPUT (0, ERR=40) @(5,K), A,
45 LET A$ = STR(A:"0000")
50 IF LEN(A$) > 4 GO TO 185
55 INPUT (0, ERR=55) @(17,K), B$
60 IF LEN(A$) > 10 GO TO 195
65 INPUT (0, ERR=65) @(30,K), C
70 LET C$ = STR(A:"0000")
75 IF LEN(C$) > 4 GO TO 205
80 INPUT (0, ERR=80) @(42,K), D
```

Notes from MAI Basic Four training, BASIC program listing (1976)

This was typically due to having disk drives in a dirty environment, or maintenance had not been performed, or dirty disk packs were inserted. My employment at MAI was for a period of twenty months or so. During this period, there were several new computer announcements. Memory and storage capacity was increasing dramatically and the overall aesthetic of computers and monitors was beginning to look more streamlined.

Friends and fellow graduates of mine had found employment in other, similar companies. Each of these companies was a manufacturer of computers and they each implemented their computers in a unique, proprietary format. There were commonalities amongst the manufacturers since minicomputer technology was becoming fairly standard by this time. Bits and bytes were standard, but how they were arranged and accessed in the hardware of the computer was the differentiator among the manufacturers.

Minicomputer companies were competing with one another for business, therefore any edge in speed and performance was hyped up and marketed. These performance advantages were also proprietary to each of the companies. Computer architecture differences between manufacturers were sufficient enough to make peripheral devices incompatible between these companies.

Once a small business decided on a manufacturers' computer system, it was essentially locked into that computer company for upgrades, add-on peripherals, expansion modules, and software. This is how large computer companies maintained their clientele in this era. The operating systems that ran on each of these computer systems were also different between the manufacturers. Therefore, a small business would be locked into the computer company for many years after their initial computer investment.

Many small companies would be tempted to poach employees from the manufacturers of their computers. For example, a small business would often hire a computer company technician that had already acquired all the training necessary, to maintain their computer systems. Computer technicians were in high demand and many of us switched employers fairly often.

I joined a smaller company after leaving MAI in 1978. The position offered to me was chief technologist for the company. The position also involved periodic traveling across Canada. My new employer, **DATAPHARM,** had developed an innovative pharmaceutical profile system where pharmacies could access a centralized database of patient profiles. The patient profiles were used to administer prescriptions. This software and hardware was unique and ground-breaking at the time. It was exciting to join this company as it would involve having my own laboratory and test equipment. As part of the new role, I would also breadboard circuit designs and test them, as well as working directly with the chief engineer of the company. Extremely enthusiastic and proud of this new position, I recall frequently working late since the satisfaction derived was exceptional. As time progressed, more responsibilities were handed to me.

I also acted as a liaison between suppliers of computer equipment and this company. This role taught me how to source small electronic components. Other benefits included having the freedom to devise new methods of work, to purchase new test equipment, and to enhance my laboratory. This position was ideal, as it embraced many of the subjects taught to me in my college education. Since computer uptime was critical to this type of health-related business, I also learned how to work under pressure. The pharmaceutical patient profile computer systems had to be running 24 hours a day, 7 days a week.

The computer systems that provided the patient profile service at this small company were acquired from a different computer manufacturer than MAI. As mentioned earlier, small businesses would select one manufacturer for all their computer equipment. Because of this, it was necessary for me to learn the software and hardware of these new computers. The manufacturer, a large US company, **Data General,** was fairly ubiquitous in the minicomputer world. Data General was a few sizes larger than my previous employer, **MAI**. Data General also maintained a centralized training center, located in Massachusetts.

After working at **DATAPHARM** for a few weeks, it was suggested to attend some formal training courses for their Data General computer systems. By this time, I was familiar with training environments and felt comfortable with the decision to acquire training. I headed off and spent two weeks learning and becoming familiar with Data General hardware and software. This manufacturer training was expensive as food and lodging also had to be considered. Costs ran into the thousands of dollars.

The knowledge gained was priceless and the training was fairly intensive. Upon returning, I had a head full of new information and all the manuals, books and notes that were provided with the training. I worked at this job for two years or so. While occasionally traveling across Canada in this new role, many new friendships and acquaintances were struck up. DATAPHARM had smaller satellite offices in other provinces, where each office had its own computer equipment to be maintained.

Each office would periodically be visited to maintain the equipment, implement new hardware and to diagnose problems. In this two-year period, my familiarization increased with computer equipment from the computer maker, Data General.

At the age of 23, with intimate knowledge of computer systems from two large minicomputer makers, it felt like I was on top of the world. My spare time was also spent dabbling in microcomputer technology and following advancements in the fast-paced microcomputer world. It can be said that I lived and breathed computers during this era and recall wanting to discuss computers at every opportunity. People were captivated by computer technology and the rapid advancements that were occurring in this era. Computer technicians were held in high regard as the mystique of computers grew. This was long before the modern day PC and home computers. Computer technology was evolving at a fast pace.

My close friends and colleagues were also involved in technology related work and we would catch up on what we were doing at get togethers. We often compared jobs and the perks each of us enjoyed in our respective positions. We also shared industry gossip and news of any interesting new job opportunities. Usually, we would share new job opportunities only after having applied for a position. Career advancement was just as important as job satisfaction in this early phase of our careers.

In 1979, a friend approached me about purchasing a used microcomputer system. He had owned this particular system for two years and could never find time to get it running correctly. Much of it was still in kit form. The microcomputer was an **IMSAI 8080**, the same microcomputer I had been reading about for a few years. Needless to say, the opportunity was seized and the IMSAI 8080 purchased. Countless hours of my spare time were then spent attempting to understand the microcomputer architecture and the S-100 bus of this system. The S-100 bus was how peripheral cards plugged into the backplane of the microcomputer and interfaced with one another.

Fortunately, access to an oscilloscope through my employment as a technician came in handy. After reading and rereading manuals and experimenting, I managed to get the microcomputer running. It was a fairly primitive set up, however, and it was necessary for any binary code to be hand-toggled in through front panel switches. Although this was a nice challenge, the micro did not really perform much with the memory and I/O cards purchased with it. Memory was limited to an insignificant 4k bytes. The microcomputer was shelved a year later with the thought of upgrading it at a later date. New and more powerful S-100 based interface cards were being regularly introduced although costs were still prohibitive.

IMSAI 8080 Microcomputer with toggle switches and lamps (1976)

It was mentioned earlier how clients poached employees from large computer makers, this also occurred in the other direction. While employed at DATAPHARM, the opportunity often arose to meet with sales and support people from Data General, the manufacturer of our computer systems. I had also received technical training at the Data General facilities in the US.

It was after a two year period at DATAPHARM that I was approached by a technician from Data General. He suggested that I look into a job opening that had just become available. Employees of companies often received referral fees to find suitable candidates for job openings and I found out this would be a referral. The opportunity was secretly looked into by meeting with a manager at Data General. After some careful consideration, a decision was made to accept an offer of employment.

This was a difficult decision for me since my current technologist position met my needs very well. Ambition and career advancement took over in the decision. Much greater opportunity for advancement was available through the Data General Corporation. I had decided this was best for me and my future. Data General was a powerhouse of a computer company and was growing by leaps and bounds in the late 1970s and early 1980s. The offer also included considerable training on new computer systems. It was an offer that could not be refused.

My new role began shortly afterwards and after working alongside other Data General technicians, I was sent away for eight weeks of training in the summer of 1980. The location of the training was Dallas, Texas where much of the summer was spent. Data General had a large laboratory and training center set up which catered to our every need. While on training, we lived in company housing where a flat was shared with another employee.

Upon my return from training, work began at the new position. My position was designated as Field Service Engineer. I usually worked on my own, unless the problem was critical and a solution was not in sight. A second level engineer would then be sent to assist me. This position was much like my first job with MAI, except of course the hardware and software were different.

Both MAI and Data General computer systems were minicomputer based. At this stage of my career, I had already acquired a very good reputation as a reliable and successful Field Service Engineer. There were a few accounts to maintain and look after. After a year or so, larger and more prestigious accounts were handed to me.

NOVA®LINE COMPUTERS
Instruction Reference Card

DataGeneral
Engineering Publications Department
Southboro, Massachusetts   01772

© Data General Corporation 1975
All rights reserved
NOVA and SUPERNOVA are registered trademarks of
Data General Corporation

Data General Instruction Reference Card (1978)

These accounts were considered critical, which meant that downtime was to be kept to a minimum as per contractual terms. It was necessary to quickly respond if a computer system at these particular accounts was down for any length of time.

My employment at the Data General position lasted six years. Within two years, I was asked about relocating to Ottawa. There had been an opening, and Ottawa was not far from my home base of Montreal. I had some family living in Ottawa at this time, so the decision was not very difficult. After moving to Ottawa, I worked for Data General (Ottawa) for a period of four years.

During the four-year period with Data General (Ottawa), many challenges were encountered. I was in a new city and had left all my friends behind. This new freedom allowed me to explore and expand my base of knowledge. It was always in my mind to pursue a Computer Science program, and soon evening school classes began at a local university. This had been a path I always intended to follow and the evening classes offered at this university were appealing. A new programming language had been developed around this time, **Pascal**. Pascal was designed as a teaching language for students to learn structured, compiled programming. It was unlike the previous interpreter language I had studied, BASIC. The local university offered a course in Pascal as part of the first year of a Computer Science program. I enrolled at Carleton University in 1983.

```
09:06 MAY 14 '83 CHECKSOLUTION.CEFILES
PROGRAM CheckAccount (Input, Output);
{ A program to process a single checking account.
  Assignment #4 CE 177.
  Input file is called INFILE.CEFILES             }
TYPE
    IdRange = 11111 .. 99999;
VAR
    StartBal, CurBal : Real;
    AccountId : IdRange;

PROCEDURE ReadHeader (VAR AccountId : IdRange;
                      VAR StartBal : Real);
{ Reads account header and month              }
CONST
    StringSize = 20;
VAR
    Name, Month : Char;
    I : Integer;
BEGIN
    { Read and print name   }
    FOR I := 1 TO StringSize DO
        BEGIN
            Read (Name);
            Write (Name)
        END; {FOR}

    { Read account Id number and starting balance }
    Read (AccountId, StartBal);
    Readln;
    Writeln ('Account No. ', AccountId: 5);

    { Read and print month   }
    WHILE NOT Eoln DO
        BEGIN
```

Pascal programming language listing, Carleton University (1983)

This new chapter in my life was fairly exciting. I was in a new city, had a new job position, and in the evenings was studying my favorite subject. The decision was made to also enroll in a second computer course, increasing my university studies up to four evenings of classes per week. The workload, however, was too demanding when combined with my day job. This particular university had a Computer Science program set up for evening studies. The first two years of the three-year program could be completed in the evenings, but the final or third year of studies would need to be completed during the day.

Carleton University Comp. Science program, student card (1983)

The next two years of my life were fairly intensive. I was determined to work towards a Computer Science degree. While employed at Data General, other computer languages were explored. A small, portable computer, **DG/One**, would often be brought home from work to learn how to program in Assembler. Incidentally, the DG/One portable computer was the world's first laptop computer, introduced in 1984!

Assembler language was a step up from directly coding a computer in machine code through the front panel. The machine code was created by a program compiled in Assembler. My manager took notice of my determination to learn software and ensured that I would be enrolled in any software related training that became available.

In 1982, it was decided to upgrade the IMSAI 8080 microcomputer purchased a few years earlier. The IMSAI 8080 had until this time been a work in progress. In 1982-83, it was discovered that completing my university programming assignments on a home computer was possible if one was available. Allowing students to use their own computers was a forward-looking step taken by the university to become part of the new, growing PC based world.

I was now motivated to bring my IMSAI 8080 up to modern standards of memory and CPU power. New, more powerful processor boards and larger main memory were researched, and several of these new boards were purchased and assembled. The boards were purchased as blank circuit boards with a collection of active and discrete components. Assembling them all together was a considerable challenge and my technical background was instrumental in getting this done. With access to test equipment, weeks were spent troubleshooting the IMSAI 8080 backplane with the newer I/O boards in place. With upgrades, the IMSAI 8080 would now have dual Z-80 microprocessors and an increase in main memory up to a whopping 64 Kbytes. At the time, a popular microcomputer operating system called CP/M was standard for S-100 based micros. A copy was purchased and the process of getting it all running was begun. It was probably six months later that I finally succeeded in bootstrapping the computer from floppy disks to where CP/M took over and ran it. The moment of seeing the CP/M prompt on my computer terminal was euphoric. Moments like this become engraved in our minds! From that day on, I was able to work on my university assignments from home.

My position as Field Service Engineer was primarily a hardware-oriented job, where computer problems were diagnosed and then repaired. By 1984, I had been working with hardware for a period of eight years since graduating from college. I began to see how quickly hardware evolved and how difficult it was to keep up with new and more powerful computer equipment. The diagnostic process had also become much more complex. Diagnostics began to be detached from hardware and discrete components could no longer be replaced. The replacements were now called FRU or **Field Replaceable Unit**. With rapid service in mind, computers began to be assembled in modules. The early days of isolating computer problems down to a computer chip had completely ended. We were instructed to replace these larger FRU modules and have the FRU sent to a repair depot afterwards. The complexity of the FRU had precluded us from any sort of field repairs. Computer systems complexity was also increasing.

A CAREER

Complex memory mapping schemes had become popular. A small physical memory address was mapped into a much larger memory array through a virtual addressing scheme. In only a few short years, the amount of accessible physical memory in a typical minicomputer system had grown by leaps and bounds. Soon, wide address buses were common where large memory arrays could be mapped directly. This technical advancement dramatically increased both memory access times and computer performance.

The period from the early 1980s to the mid-1980s brought rapid change to the computer industry. Minicomputer systems were becoming larger and more complex year over year. The term "super mini" was coined in 1983 or so. One of the last computer systems I was trained on at Data General was the revolutionary 64 bit **MV/8000**. This was one of the so-called "super minis" where this new large computer class functioned like a small mainframe. The MV/8000 story can be read in The **Soul of A New Machine** book by Tracy Kidder. These "super mini" computers were marketed to large corporations where computer uptime had become critical. Computer maintenance had to be scheduled, usually in the overnight period. When these new computer systems failed, technicians assigned to the account were under immense pressure to get the computer system up and running. We were measured on how quickly we could diagnose and repair problems on these large systems.

Smaller computer systems were still common, but the criticality of computer uptime had become a new competitive yardstick in the computer industry. Computer manufacturers were ranked on the reliability of their computers. In the 1984 era, I began to notice that computer software had become a large part of large computer purchases. Software evolved to where small to medium sized companies could purchase more advanced software applications. These companies were beginning to seek turn-key solutions. Turn-key meant a company could use the hardware and the software application with little customization.

There was no longer a mystique around computer hardware. Until this time, many small companies would purchase hardware and software separately and then contract computer consultants to make it all work. Computer integrators performed the task of putting together hardware with specific software. By the mid-1980s, hardware and software applications were beginning to be bundled together at the manufacturer level. The focus was trending towards more powerful software applications. Seeing this trend unfold encouraged me to move away from hardware and seek out a software position at my employer, Data General. I had been pursuing Computer Science studies for two years and programmed small computers in my spare time. A computer software direction was becoming more interesting to me. Inquiries were made about transitioning from a Hardware Technician to a Software Support Representative. My manager at the time reassured me about receiving any available training to help with the transition. A year or so later in 1985, the transition was finally made. My new role was that of a Data General System Support Representative for both Software and Hardware. This role demanded that I work the complete solution where considerable software involvement was necessary. A few months later, I was sent on training to learn the powerful Data General Operating System **AOS/VS**.

This new position was very exciting to me at the time. My dream of working with both software and computer hardware had come to pass. Computer technology advancements were occurring at a rapid rate and it was becoming a challenge to keep up with it all. I also enjoyed working with microcomputers in my spare time and keeping up with this technology. The caveat to the new position was the continued involvement in hardware maintenance at my client accounts. This did not concern me at the time due to the excitement of working with computer software in my job. Throughout my employment at Data General, many awards were won as well as performance bonuses received.

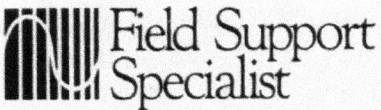

Data General Field Support Specialist, business card (1984)

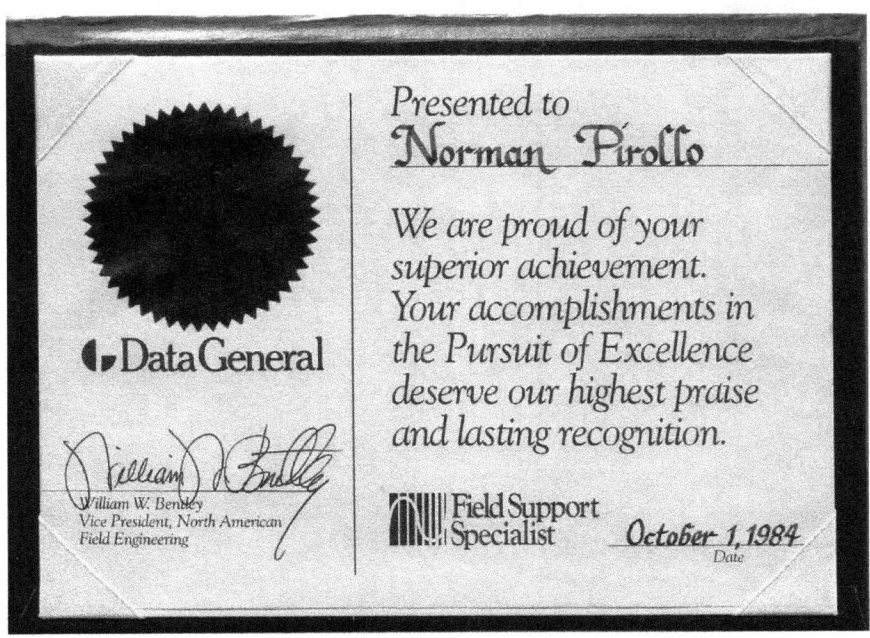

Data General Excellence Award, prestigious award won in 1984

My university studies had also been completed during this time. The decision was made not to continue on to a third year of Computer Science studies since this involved leaving my job to return to school full-time. My new job had so much software involvement that I now felt fulfilled without the need to pursue a Computer Science degree. The third year of a Comp. Science degree program focused on Operating Systems. Instead of attending the day program, textbooks used in the third year of the Comp. Science program were researched and purchased. Considerable time was then invested over a few months reading and understanding operating system concepts.

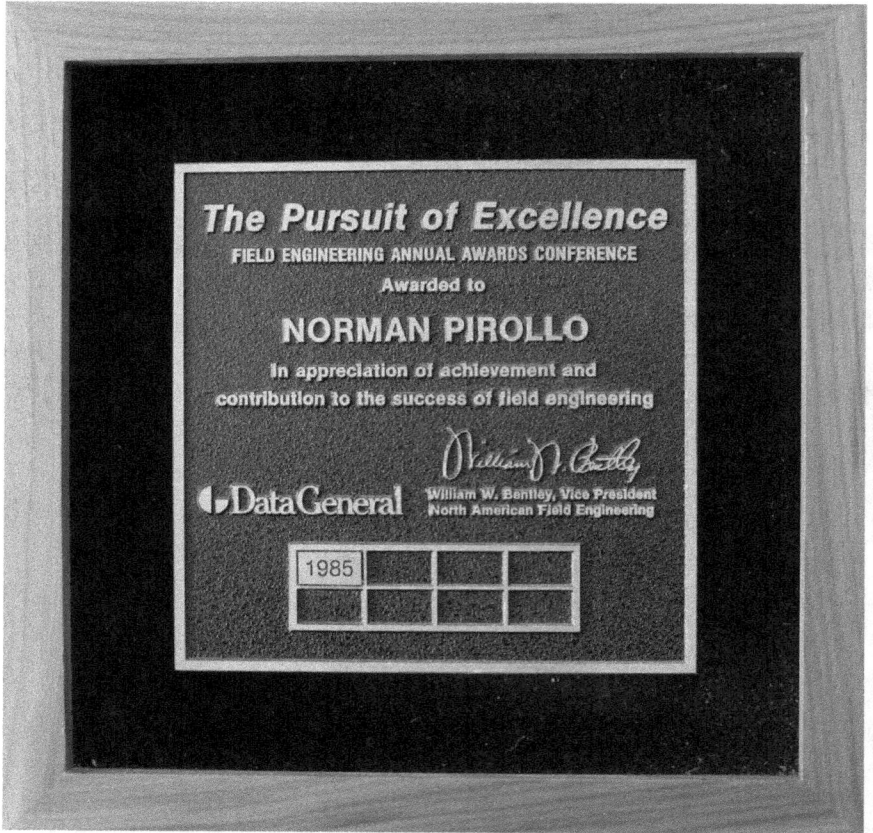

Data General Excellence Award, a prestigious award won in 1985

This new knowledge also benefitted my new role at Data General, that of supporting operating systems as a Software Support Representative. The selection of Comp. Science courses already completed helped considerably in my new software position. So much more would now be learned about software through my employer. Data General had also set up a large software training facility in Connecticut in this period. I began to attend individual courses on the Data General flagship operating system, **AOS/VS**, at the training site in Connecticut.

Interestingly, since no longer pursuing University studies and having completed putting together my IMSAI 8080 microcomputer; free time was now available to me in 1985. I found out about a part-time Woodworking Course at a local college where the course was offered once per week on Saturdays. Since helping my father out at his home workshop, an interest in woodworking had developed. There was also a need to do something creative with my hands and causing me to miss working with tools. After enrolling in this course, I began to attend once a week classes. The course itself involved the development of hand-tool skills. We were to create a project using the skills we learned while we progressed through the course.

The curriculum was based on the early European style of woodworking instruction, where hand tool skills were taught. The principle hand tools were discussed and we were shown how to hold them and taught techniques of use. The course was **Woodworking I,** the basis of any further woodworking education at the college. The project we were each asked to create was a wooden planter with dovetailed corners. The pieces of wood we used were partially prepared; they were dimensioned to rough sizes. We needed to trim the boards to accurate lengths and widths and create the corner joinery. The joinery selected was dovetails. Dovetails make an excellent mechanical joint. I looked forward to each Saturday morning class with great anticipation!

Creating a project reinforced the skills we were learning in class as well as making us feel we were progressing. The dovetailed planter was beginning to come together and each week a new tool skill would be learned.

Although this was a period of my computer career that excited me and provided great satisfaction, the weekly woodworking course stirred something in me. My career and job positions were largely service and support oriented, where I would be diagnosing hardware and software problems. Building a dovetailed planter made me realize the lack of creativity in my life. Although the planter design was already established, the process of creating a tangible object excited me and gave me purpose. I recall a similar excitement as a teenager where devices were built from surplus electronic parts as well as creating my own bicycles from components.

The woodworking course was completed and a beautiful handmade dovetailed planter was the result. There was a gleam in my eyes when I walked off with the planter at my last session and when it was shown to close friends. Being immensely proud of this accomplishment, it was decided to pursue woodworking further by enrolling in the next course in the series, **Woodworking II.** I began this course in the next semester.

Woodworking II was much more advanced; we progressed from hand tools to using machines and larger woodworking equipment as well as using hand tools. The Woodworking II course was also project-oriented. While learning new skills, we were tasked with building a small cabinet. The components of the cabinet were more complex than the dovetailed planter and began to approximate furniture. Woodworking II was also part-time with once a week classes. Looking forward to each class, I was excited about learning to use machinery and being able to create wood parts with the machinery. Both these courses were part of the Cabinetmaking curriculum at the community college. At the time, the plan was to gradually work towards a Cabinetmaking Diploma in my free time.

Dovetailed planter from Woodworking I (1985); still in use today.

I completed this course and continued with the next course in the series. The next course, **Cabinetmaking**, combined many of the skills learned in the previous courses. We went further in machine use and techniques as well as learning new skills. The course also involved a group project. This project was far more complex than the projects in the previous courses. The project was a roll-top desk and students were divided into small groups. Each of these groups was tasked with creating components for the roll-top desk. There would be one roll top desk built as a class project by all the students in the course.

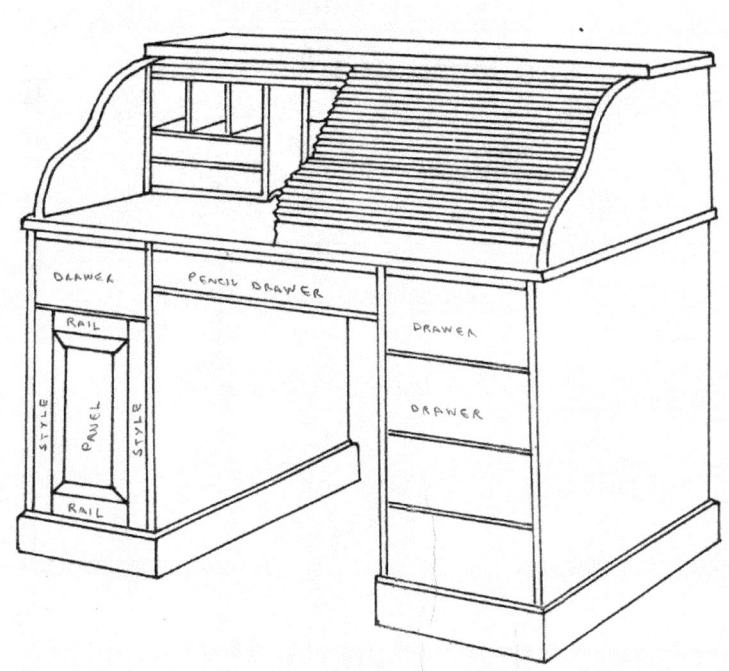

Oak roll-top desk created in Cabinetmaking class (1985).

After completing these three woodworking courses, I went no further in my woodworking studies. My energy was instead channeled back into my computer career. In early 1986, I was informed of an opening at another large computer firm with a satellite office in Ottawa.

The company was larger than my current employer, Data General. Friends of mine also worked for this larger company, **DEC** or Digital Equipment Corporation. Although content at working for Data General, I was open to new opportunities. This was an era where it was expected of employees to regularly seek better opportunities. Companies understood this and offered enticements to join.

A CAREER

While employed at Data General, an interview was arranged with Digital Equipment Corporation or **DEC** in the spring of 1986. The new position at DEC would provide me greater responsibility, which included the managing of my own training. The position was exclusively a software position whereas my current job was a combination of hardware and software. There would be a component of travel across Canada with this new position, and my title would be Regional Support Representative. I mulled the offer over for a few weeks.

Digital Equipment Corp. (DEC) had given me three weeks to decide. In this period, I was sent on training for Data General. It was hardware training and it was during this training that the DEC offer was given very serious consideration. Considerable thought was given to the rapid evolution in computer hardware. Computer systems were far more complex than only a few years earlier. The complexity removed my connection with hardware. Discrete components were now replaced by larger FRU modules. I began to see my future and it was no longer as challenging to be in computer hardware. The decision was made to make a clean break and only work with software. After accepting the DEC offer, I flew back from a shortened training course to officially resign from Data General after a successful six years.

My new career at Digital Equipment Corp. (DEC) began in early July 1986. Over the next weeks and months, my immersion into company training occurred. DEC computer architecture was somewhat different from Data General's. The I/O of the system was handled differently. Having already worked on different minicomputer systems; the differences in DEC PDP-11 computer architecture warranted considerable training. Aside from an initial week of hardware training, the majority of courses were software courses. My initial role at DEC would be to support a real-time operating system called RSX. This was a high performance OS and the PDP-11 computers it ran on were typically installed in demanding, process control environments. The OS itself was not very complex, but was radically different from any of the operating systems I had previously worked on.

RSX was largely an interrupt-driven OS, which ensured rapid response times to peripheral device input (real-time processing). This was in direct comparison to mainstream operating systems of the era used in general-purpose timeshare computing.

The new position at DEC began to demand a considerable amount of my time and the learning curve was steep. I had to learn RSX and feel confident enough in my knowledge to travel around Canada in a support role. This was to be my first computer employment that involved software work exclusively. Not wanting to fail at the job, RSX OS was studied even in my spare time. This dedication and focus to my job precluded any time for hobbies or pastimes. My interest in woodworking was temporarily shelved as it was necessary to be successful at my new position.

Two years went by and the job evolved. There was change at DEC and RSX support was beginning to wane. By 1988, I was not nearly as busy as I had been in 1986. DEC was also beginning to embrace a new operating system, **UNIX**. New support centers were being created to be able to support UNIX. These support centers needed staffing and an offer was presented to transition me to a UNIX support role. There was not much choice in the matter as my RSX role was slowly fading away. The UNIX OS was another in a series of operating systems necessary to be learned. Within a ten year period, I had already worked with software from MAI, Data General and two different operating systems at DEC.

In this period, I also studied and taught myself Assembler and CP/M, a microcomputer **Operating System** (OS). This was aside from my (Pascal) studies in the Computer Science program at University. For the next months and years, I weaned myself away from RSX and immersed myself in the UNIX operating system. As part of my UNIX learning, 'C' language programming also had to be understood since UNIX was written in 'C'. In 1988-89, I enrolled in two different 'C' programming courses at the same local community college where my woodworking had been studied a few years earlier.

UNIX was radically different from other mainstream operating systems. In that era, a few computer companies began to offer UNIX as an operating system platform, but only reluctantly. UNIX was considered an **Open Source** operating system and therefore not proprietary in nature. Large companies could not profit as much from UNIX sales. UNIX was offered as an Operating System (OS) through DEC but only if a customer demanded it. It was later revealed that it was not marketed nearly as much as the flagship, proprietary operating system VMS. Nonetheless, this was an exciting period of my life.

UNIX support people were in the minority at DEC and so we had carte blanche to pursue any training necessary to do our job. After many years of supporting a variety of proprietary operating systems, it dawned on me that these operating systems were inseparable from the hardware manufacturer. Proprietary operating systems were optimized for the manufacturer's hardware. This translated to performance gains since the OS would take full advantage of the computer hardware. As well, computer makers of this era profited greatly from proprietary operating systems. This became a liability since each time I moved to a new hardware platform, it became necessary to learn a new operating system. The UNIX OS was different in that it was designed to be portable on different hardware platforms. UNIX was considered to be "Open Source" software.

One of a series of UNIX courses, Ultrix-32 Internals (1987)

The advantage for a client would be that their investment in UNIX could be ported to another hardware platform. The disadvantage with UNIX portability meant that the OS would not be optimized for specific computer platforms. The manufacturers were addressing this with versions of UNIX specific to their hardware. One might say that this defeated the purpose of UNIX, but a large part of the core UNIX OS was written as a generic operating system. The DEC version of UNIX was called **ULTRIX** and this is what I now supported.

With this in mind, it became obvious that by supporting UNIX and learning as much as possible about the UNIX OS, my skills would be just as portable as UNIX. It would then be possible to join another computer maker and support their version of UNIX. This critical point had great appeal to me. After many years of learning and re-learning specific manufacturer software, I became highly motivated to learn UNIX.

The ULTRIX support role continued for a few years. Two years after my support of ULTRIX began; DEC opened a support center in Ottawa. As a member of this new support center, my role was in the support of the ULTRIX operating system. The support group was fairly small in comparison to the much larger flagship VMS group. It was an exciting period; there were not many ULTRIX clients at this time and it allowed me to invest time into learning the ULTRIX operating system. Whenever a new position was begun, I immersed myself in the software necessary to support it. This new role demanded my complete dedication and focus.

Norman Pirollo
System Support Specialist
Customer Technology Support Centre

Digital Equipment of Canada Limited
200, boulevard de la Technologie
Hull (Quebec) J8Z 3H6
Telephone (819) 772-7173
Fax (819) 772-7036

Digital Equipment Corp. System Support Specialist (1989)

I also travelled and had the opportunity to meet with many clients in my new support role. The site visits also allowed me to view ULTRIX systems in practical applications. Each client utilized the ULTRIX system for a different application, and this became my introduction to the business use of UNIX computers. This experience was rewarding and the exposure gained made it possible to understand the client's business. The business exposure would be invaluable to me a few years later. The ULTRIX operating system evolved into the much larger and more powerful OSF/1 operating system. OSF/1 followed current industry standards for UNIX at the time.

Since clients were now seeking standardization and software portability, it was in the best interest of computer companies to offer industry standard variants of UNIX. The OSF/1 operating system would be a transitional OS. DEC was developing the Digital UNIX operating system where it would be their flagship UNIX operating system. I continued to support these DEC versions of UNIX for many years. The OS had evolved into a full operating system and had become mainstream in this period. DEC had begun to offer a large suite of applications that had been ported to Digital UNIX.

In the 1992 timeframe, I purchased and moved into a new home. At this point in my career, supporting UNIX in my job position was fairly stress-free. More of my spare time was spent working on my newly acquired home. Walls were put up in the basement and the home made more livable. There was a fairly large basement available to me and it was enjoyable spending time at home.

Thought was given to taking up a hobby since I had fond memories of the woodworking courses followed a few years earlier. Until this time, my career had been a priority and woodworking was placed on the back burner. With little time available to indulge in woodworking, my subscriptions to two woodworking magazines continued. Taking up woodworking as a hobby occasionally crossed my mind.

With my new home and a large basement available, some room was finally available to be able to pursue woodworking. Within a year of moving in to the new home, an investment was made in some woodworking tools. A small bench was set up in one small corner of the basement. After purchasing a very good band saw, I slowly began to work on very small, simple projects. This caused me to get excited about woodworking again. It had been approximately six years since working on a woodworking project. More wood and tools were purchased in the next months.

Creative Discovery

"Happiness lies in the joy of achievement and the thrill of creative effort"

Franklin D. Roosevelt

THE YEAR 1992 WAS the midpoint of my career at DEC. My employment at DEC had begun in 1986 and my final year of employment was to be 1996. I had now become a UNIX Support Representative. The current position involved considerably less travel, where the only travel was for training purposes. The company had a team of representatives located at each satellite office that were sent to customer sites when necessary. My role was to provide phone support to these representatives. We had a small lab facility where I could test new versions of software and applications. We would also test upcoming (Beta) versions of software on dedicated in-house computers. A large part of my work was to provide technical assistance to Digital employees and clients, performed over the phone.

UNIX had become commercialized by this time. It began as a radical, alternative operating system, almost on the fringe. Due to its "open source" origins, it was becoming increasingly popular. Large companies such as DEC had their own versions of UNIX and offered full support. Small businesses were no longer skeptical about the reliability of UNIX-based operating systems.

I was a member of a team supporting UNIX. Within DEC, UNIX had evolved from ULTRIX to OSF/1 and by 1993 to Digital UNIX. The operating system had become very reliable and DEC released occasional version upgrades that contained software fixes. There were also patch kits available that addressed critical, time-sensitive issues.

My UNIX support group was fairly small within the larger support center. In this period, my focus was exclusively on supporting UNIX or a UNIX-derived operating system. I appreciated that UNIX was portable. The majority of software reps. in the support center supported the flagship VMS operating system. No longer motivated to learn yet another operating system, there was no interest in supporting VMS at this point in my career. In the past sixteen years of employment, I had already worked on many different, proprietary systems. My niche was with UNIX and I could easily leave DEC to work at another company to support their version of UNIX.

In light of this, my career ambitions began to wane. I felt secure in my employment at DEC. There were occasional discussions with my manager about a career path and we discussed options. Usually, a management role was mentioned. DEC encouraged the promotion of people from within for many of its management positions. This was an option I could pursue. It was, however, not appealing as my technical role continued to be rewarding. By maintaining a technical role, I could leave DEC and easily seek employment elsewhere as a UNIX Support Rep. On the other hand, by joining management it would be somewhat more difficult to leave and join another company as a manager.

This was a crossroad in my career. I continued to enjoy my role in UNIX support although concerns began to enter my mind regarding my future. The software support role began to be very demanding, constant updating of skills was necessary. To remain competitive, large companies such as DEC would often release new versions of operating systems with new functionality. New versions had features that the competition often did not have.

A client would often select one computer vendor over another for a unique characteristic of the operating system. Therefore, software support reps. including me would need to constantly update themselves on these new features. New applications would also be announced on a regular basis and we were expected to support these applications. We were occasionally sent on training for new, more complex software but were also expected to teach ourselves a large part of it.

At the same time, work on a small woodworking workspace in the basement of my new home continued while working at DEC. Often, a few hours would be spent in the evening and weekends tinkering in my shop space. By this time, a temporary bench had been assembled and a small assortment of tools accumulated.

The year 1993 was a seminal year for me. Although enjoying my job, it would be my woodworking that began to excite me. In casual conversations with people, my woodworking hobby was often mentioned. Talk of my day job as a UNIX Support Rep. would be secondary. In this period, I began to feel both content and confused at the same time. The satisfaction derived from setting up my woodworking space was greater than the enjoyment derived from my job.

Soon, the need arose to enclose the workspace where I had been woodworking in my basement. A side effect of woodworking is the unavoidable generation of dust. It became necessary to enclose this new workspace to contain dust and to keep it from infiltrating the rest of the basement area. The furnace area was of particular concern. Research began on building an enclosed workshop. Three walls would be built and a door installed. The new workshop would be approximately 14 feet X 16 feet in size. Soon work began on this project in the evenings and on weekends. Having never done this type of construction, there would be considerable research on how to build interior walls and frame a door. The walls would also need to have drywall surfaces to seal them from the rest of the basement.

Once the workshop was completed, additional woodworking machines would be purchased. This necessitated the installation of dedicated power outlets in the workshop. Additional outlets were necessary where each outlet was to have its own dedicated circuit and circuit breaker. This configuration allowed me to install machines that draw high current and would not trip their circuit breakers while starting. This was accomplished by studying the electrical code on how to install and route electrical wiring and circuit breakers. After researching the necessary amount of light per square foot of workshop space, four banks of overhead fluorescent lamps were installed in the space. The amount of light produced was now more than sufficient. Lighting is fairly inexpensive to install.

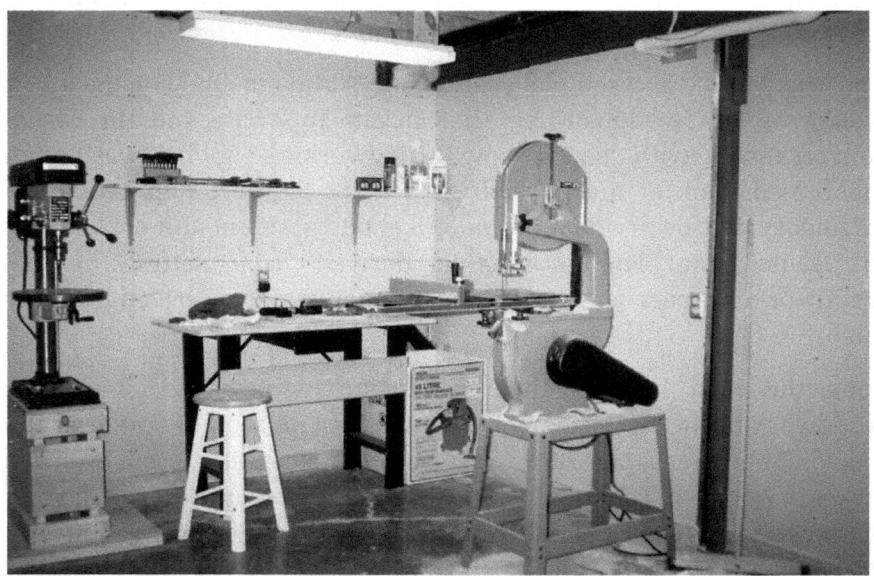

Newly completed workshop with new band saw, drill press and temporary workbench (1994)

Work progressed on this new workshop area and a few weeks later the framing was completed and drywalled with a door installed. My confidence was high that this workshop would contain the dust generated by my woodworking. The workshop was beginning to look like a professional installation!

CREATIVE DISCOVERY 59

Upon completion of the workshop, the electrical work would need to be inspected. I arranged to have this done and it passed with flying colors. This effort was very rewarding!

After completing the workshop, the walls surrounding the workspace were found to be somewhat confining. The workshop was away from a window and without natural light. It was decided to install a large window on one of the external walls of the workshop to draw light in from the naturally lit basement. Next, research was performed on how to install a window. The first step would be to purchase an appropriately sized and well-sealed window. An opening in the wall was created and a window successfully installed. This proved to be a wise move as I could now tap into natural light from the other part of the basement.

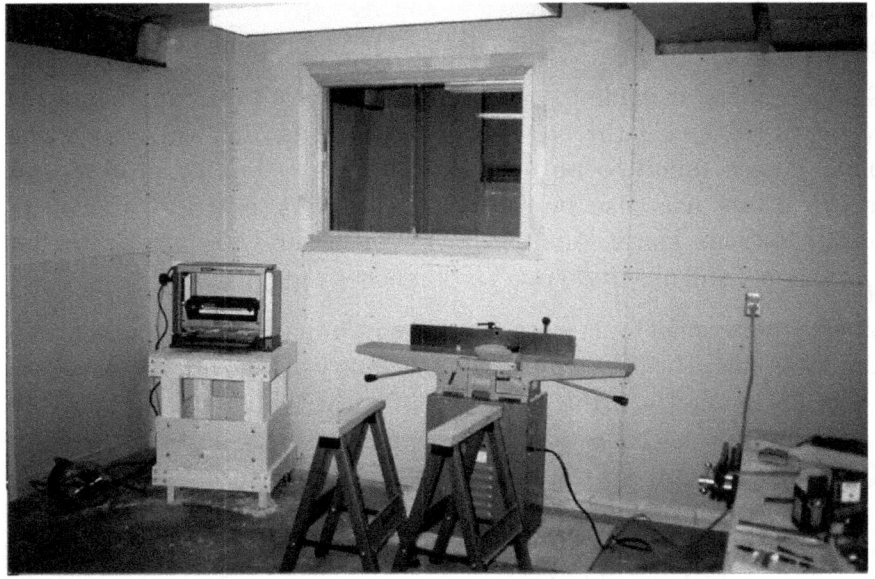

Newly completed workshop with view through add-on window. Also seen are new jointer and thickness planer (1994)

After completing the new workshop, the decision was made not to do much more in the new workshop for a period of weeks. I would refocus on my work instead. This period also provided me the opportunity to make plans for this new workshop space.

Changes to the Digital Equipment (DEC) implementation of UNIX were coming fast and furious over the next while. I would need to invest considerable time in upgrading my technical knowledge. This was performed by attending training and reading technical announcements oriented towards support staff like myself.

However, I kept thinking about my new workshop and began to plan the purchase of a table saw and a portable thickness planer. At least one sturdy workbench was also necessary. Early in 1994, preparations were made to build a workbench. Often, woodworking preoccupied my mind at work. The Internet was in its infancy and I had access to a primitive search engine, **Mosaic**, at my workplace. My lunch hour was often spent reading online articles about setting up woodworking shops. A few magazines and a book that discussed this topic were also purchased. My imagination was sparked after reading a magazine article. It was a straightforward design for a workbench with drawers.

The decision was made to build this workbench; the components and wood were then gathered. Shortly afterwards, the workbench was built. It was found to be not very difficult to build and a second, identical one was also built. They were very practical as well as having storage space. Along with much larger workbenches in my workshop, I still use these two workbenches today!

Slowly, more small tools were purchased along with a thickness planer and table saw. These two pieces of machinery along with the band saw I already owned are the mainstay of most woodworking shops. A rudimentary dust collection network was also set up to gather dust and wood chips from the machines. Since the workshop was fairly small, it became important to not have clutter and especially not to have a dusty environment. An overhead airborne dust collector was also built which would clean the shop air every few minutes. The workshop was now looking great and I was ready to begin woodworking.

CREATIVE DISCOVERY   61

Workshop with new workbenches, ceiling air cleaner, wall cabinet and new table saw (1994)

The process of building a workshop and outfitting it invigorated me. Since more time would be spent in my new workshop, I gained new excitement in my life and did not mind my job as much. New projects such as frame and panel doors and small boxes were also begun. The very first box created in my workshop was very rudimentary. In hindsight, I felt the need to complete a first simple project to gain confidence in progressing to more complex projects. My UNIX support role was also growing and I was given greater responsibility. My team had regular meetings with the manager at the time, and we were often tasked with looking after specific client accounts. These were high profile accounts and it was in the business interest of DEC to assign a dedicated support representative to address issues these clients might have. These higher profile customers also paid to have premium support, where we would provide them a higher priority when their computer system failed.

It was late in 1994 that interest in my work began to gradually erode. I had attained a level of competence where my work was no longer as challenging to me as it once was. Although my skills would regularly be updated to keep up with the latest software versions supported, this was no longer a challenge. It was increasingly obvious that there was no further advancement possible in my current role. The alternative was to switch to a management track, however, this had no appeal to me. I wanted to remain in a software role and not lose my technical edge. The team I was a member of offered little to no possibility for advancement. The team had remained the same in size for a period of years while the flagship VMS group grew by leaps and bounds. I definitely had no interest in supporting VMS.

With all this in mind, I turned to my growing hobby of woodworking for fulfillment. Small projects of mine were occasionally brought in to my workplace to show colleagues. Examples of this were small band saw boxes. These are boxes that are completely cut out of a block of wood using a band saw.

The very first boxes I ever made. Band sawn boxes (1994)

Slowly, I began to realize that the process of creating excited me. New skills were being learned as well as applying them. The knowledge gained through the woodworking courses completed a few years earlier proved to be invaluable. The courses taught me how to outfit my new workshop and which machines and tools to purchase. A need to pursue more woodworking studies was also felt. A Cabinetmaking Diploma was elusive to me; I had made strides a few years earlier to attain this goal. With this in mind, an application was made for another woodworking course at the same college attended previously. Since I already met the prerequisites, the only course available was the third level Cabinetmaking Course. This was the same course followed years ago. Upon beginning the part-time course, I was surprised to find the same instructor teaching the course that had taught the original course.

The course curriculum was exactly the same, even down to the project we were to build over the duration of the course. We were to build a roll-top desk, a fairly complex project. The class was once again divided into smaller groups, each tasked with one or more components of the desk. Since the project was the same as in the past, I dug up my old notes and handouts from the previous course. Thinking that this would save me the time of taking notes and I could instead concentrate on the lectures.

When my small group began to create the components we were tasked with, some of the pieces would not fit in with components prepared by other groups. We were scratching our heads as we had followed the handouts. After analysis, it was discovered that the instructor had slightly modified the dimensions of some roll-top desk components. This was sufficient enough to keep all the dimensioned parts from fitting together. The handouts used were from the previous course a few years back. I like to tell this story!

The Cabinetmaking program courses I completed formed the core of the program. There were a few elective courses offered which would provide enough credits to acquire a diploma. I decided to pursue one of the electives offered, a course on furniture finishes and how to apply them.

This course helped me considerably in understanding the finishing process. After leaving the Cabinetmaking program, it was felt I had the necessary knowledge to begin working on my own furniture projects. Through the Cabinetmaking program, I had become intimately familiar with many woodworking machines and learned many techniques. Rough lumber could be processed and dimensioned parts created for furniture. We were taught how to work with cut lists. It was also taught how to profile the edges of boards and how to create joinery, both simple and compound.

The year was 1995 and many thoughts were racing through my mind. The thought of a career in woodworking preoccupied my mind more. I began to read stories about other people that had transitioned from a career into woodworking. At this period in my life, I was young enough to appreciate that there were many years remaining in my computer career. It would not be wise to leave such a career and instead struggle at a woodworking career. This introspection helped me to understand myself and to newly define my goals in life. Of course, the issue of money and supporting myself was at the forefront. The current computer position at DEC compensated me very well and I was able to maintain my house, a car and also outfit my new woodworking shop. Being single at the time, my precarious financial position was clear if I were to lose my employment or quit. This motivated me to continue in my computer career and to advance my knowledge to remain relevant.

Over the next while, I continued to pursue my woodworking hobby in my spare time while working at my day job. My new workshop area continued to be outfitted with additional tools and machinery; careful not to clutter the limited space in the workshop. Having created a few band saw boxes encouraged me to create larger boxes with more traditional joinery. These would be square and rectangular boxes. I had in mind to create a series of small boxes and install music mechanisms in them. The boxes would be straightforward with hinged tops. In the early 1995 timeframe, work began on these small music boxes.

Learning Curve

"Curiosity about life in all of its aspects, I think, is still the secret of great creative people"

Leo Burnett

THE FIRST MUSIC BOXES were identical in dimensions. Through my woodworking training, I was taught to create multiple components of similar dimensions while machines were already set up. It made perfect sense to create the components for a few boxes using this method. The dimensioned pieces were small and it would not be difficult to accomplish this. After completing the boxes, music mechanisms were obtained and inserted in these boxes. Exotic woods were also used in the tops of the boxes. Woods such as lacewood would dramatically enhance the appeal of the boxes. The corner joinery was created using a jig what had been purchased.

During this time, a router table was also designed and built. The router is an important, versatile tool in the workshop. When mounted to a router table it would serve as a shaper. I then read about a popular joinery creation system in a magazine I subscribed to. The system was the Incra Jig. The jig was ordered and experiments began in its use. The box joinery and dovetail joinery created was fine, but the jig was found to be fragile. It was made of reinforced plastic and the teeth along a meshing rack system would occasionally chip off.

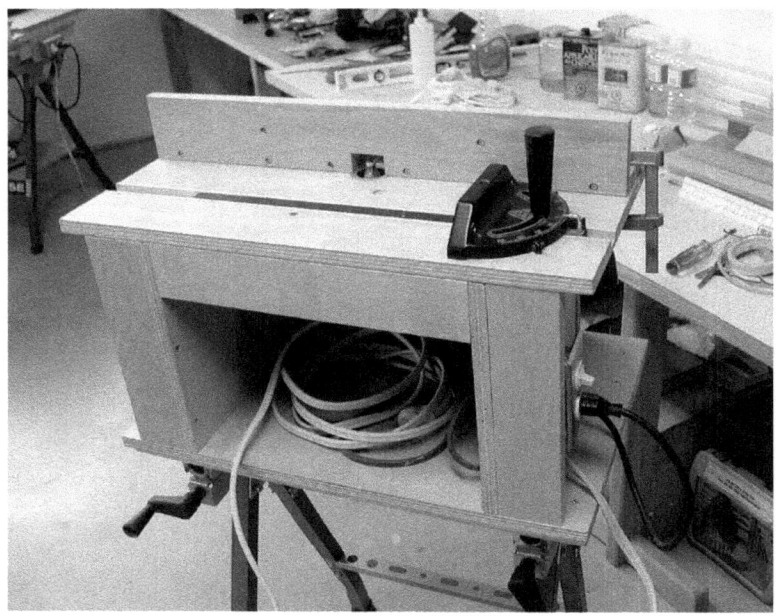

First router table designed and made for the workshop. The table had a hinged top for quick access and router bit changes (1995)

In this discovery process, the Incra Jig provided me with a taste of how advantageous these joinery jigs could be when used in conjunction with a router table. I soon returned the Incra Jig and sought an alternative system. **Incra** did have a more expensive model of joinery jig available as part of a system. After some research, it was found to have more plastic components than preferred and alternatives continued to be investigated. A competing company, **Jointech**, offered a joinery system that had very similar functionality to the Incra jig. The system was the IPM-1 system and it was constructed entirely of metal. The mechanism to advance and retract the fence was lead screw based instead of using meshing plastic teeth along a rack. From images on the Internet and in magazine ads, the mechanism was put together to be durable and to provide great accuracy. The IPM-1 joinery system was ordered, installed and then used to create small box joinery. The series of small boxes created incorporated both box and dovetail corner joinery.

After an intensive learning curve, it was straightforward to create this type of joinery using the IPM-1 jig. As with any new tool, there is a learning curve to get it right. The IPM-1 jig worked in conjunction with a series of plastic templates. The templates would be used to precisely position the fence of the jig to be able to create intricate, compound joinery. Using this type of jig made me realize that multiples of small boxes and other small products could be produced. My mind raced with the thought of making many small boxes and selling them. The sales would pay for any additional tools necessary for my workshop. This idea provided me a new option for my future. Research would need to be performed on how to market these boxes and to determine if there was an appeal for music boxes.

This was becoming a busy period in my life. I had a day job as a software support rep. along with the evolving woodworking hobby of mine. Woodworking was quickly becoming my new passion and began to fulfill a creative outlet in my life. Throughout the year 1995, work would continue on creating small boxes. The designs would slowly become more complex. What began as a straightforward box with only a hinged top soon incorporated an upper sliding compartment. The boxes had now become more practical for storing small items as well as serving as music boxes.

Over the course of the year, use of the new IPM-1 joinery jig was mastered. I recall reading the manual from cover to cover multiple times to determine if any small nuance in the operation of the IPM-1 jig was overlooked. Since the boxes created were fairly small at only about seven to eight inches in length, it was determined that solid tops and bottoms would not cause any wood movement issues. The solid tops and bottoms were fixed to the sides and the small area would preclude any wood movement. If there was wood movement, it would be very minor. From my woodworking education on wood movement, I knew that this theory would only work for very small boxes. A new approach to box building would need to be researched. Incidentally, I still have a few of these boxes twenty years later and they have not shown any cracks. They are as solid as they were when first made!

Music box with dovetail joinery made using IPM-1 jig (1995)

It became obvious that if boxes were to be marketed, small music boxes would limit my potential market. At the time, I knew it was necessary to make larger boxes. After researching my options, it was found that larger jewelry boxes were popular and a system to create these larger sized boxes was necessary. This provided me with a challenge, which I embraced. Inevitably, I would be creating larger furniture one day, and these small stepping-stones would help to achieve this goal.

A few weeks of research in the year 1995 provided me with ideas for a new series of larger boxes. These boxes would utilize floating panels for the top and bottom. The top panel would be inserted in a groove routed into each of the sides and front and back. This would allow the top panel to move slightly with the change of seasons and corresponding moisture levels. This technique would also allow me to create much larger boxes. I had moved away from music boxes around this time and instead began to focus on jewelry boxes.

The early versions created had band sawn sliding compartments located over a large compartment below. By today's standards, these early jewelry boxes were fairly crude and were as simple as can be. The tops were attached to the carcase using hinges and a brass chain kept the top from going too far back when open. I experimented with different woods and combinations of woods to determine what was most aesthetically appealing. Some woods were more difficult to work with than others, but this obstacle was easily overcome since machines were used to create these boxes.

After creating a few different boxes, the box designs were shown to friends and family to get their opinion. They were asked to be honest about what they saw; were the boxes appealing and practical. The feedback received was overwhelmingly positive and this encouraged me to work further on the designs. I divided my time between my work and my woodworking hobby throughout the year. By year end 1995, a fairly large assortment of boxes of different sizes was accumulated. Each of the boxes was different from each other in wood type, as well as how the interior was arranged. The interior compartments were now assembled from small, thin pieces of wood instead of band sawing through one large, monolithic piece of wood. This refined the aesthetic of the boxes and they began to have a more professional look.

My job kept me busy; as well the UNIX customer base at DEC was growing. The support team I was part of was quite busy. DEC also offered new support plans for larger clients where downtime was to be minimized considerably. The work involved rotating support in the evenings and on weekends. Each team member would work an after-hours shift and carry a portable phone with them to quickly respond to a client. This was a new demand placed on my team, but we managed it between us. Members of my team were senior people, each with considerable experience. We could easily manage ourselves without difficulty. Our manager at the time appreciated that we each had numerous years of expertise in our field and would leave us to make our own decisions on how to provide support. Time marched on and 1995 turned into early 1996.

The box making was progressing very well and serious consideration was given to the marketing of these boxes. There were two colleagues at work that enjoyed woodworking, and we would often have conversations about tools, techniques and where to source wood. An opportunity arose when a colleague introduced me to a wood supplier. I proceeded to purchase a few pickup truck loads of locally harvested maple and walnut at excellent prices. Some of the wood was highly figured birds' eye maple. This was also to be my introduction to exotic woods. The wood was in rough form, but this was not an issue since I had machines to process the planks into useable, dimensioned lumber. This purchase provided me with a great deal of wood to be used in future projects. I still retain some of this wood today!

It was no secret that I enjoyed woodworking. Enjoyment was derived when I discussed my new hobby with colleagues at work. As well, I would bring samples of interesting figured woods in to work. In the spring of 1996, a trip was made to another city, Toronto, to purchase more exotic wood. There were no suppliers of these exotics in my home city in this period. While at this large supplier, most of the wood selected was exotic and tropical. This wood was to be used to construct a more exciting series of jewelry boxes.

Since my box designs had become fairly standard by this time, the introduction of more colorful and figured woods would add to their appeal. Experiments began with cocobolo, lacewood, tiger wood, birds' eye maple and padauk. Each of these woods had unique characteristics and color. The padauk was a beautiful wood to work with but produced a fine dust when milled. Most of these exotic woods produced a fine, pervasive dust. The padauk began as a dark red wood and slowly became brown when exposed to light and air. There would be a fine red dust on the walls of my workshop whenever I worked with padauk. It became necessary to regularly sweep the dust off the walls. Whenever I switched to another species of exotic wood, the walls would change color.

LAYOFF SHOCK

"Every setback means you're one step closer to seeing the dream come to pass"

Joel Osteen

THE YEAR 1996 BEGAN as many of the previous years had begun. My software support role was fairly established by this time. My job performance was fine and expectations were often surpassed. My relations with other colleagues and managers at work were also exceptional. I continued to perform my tasks in the first months of 1996. As well, I enjoyed woodworking in my spare time.

Early in the spring of 1996 however, shocking news was delivered to me. The company, **DEC**, had begun a downsizing process. There were rapid changes occurring in the computer industry in this era. Sales of the proprietary operating system, VMS, were declining. This did not surprise me. Customers were beginning to demand open source software and UNIX was making great headway. The support center I was a member of had peaked and the company had begun to reduce the number of employees. A considerable amount of the support work was being shifted to US Support Centers. It made economic sense for the company to consolidate its support in fewer locations. Although I was supporting the popular Digital UNIX OS, DEC had also decided to shift support of Digital UNIX to larger US support centers. DEC had also begun to shrink as a corporation.

Times were changing and proprietary operating systems were slowly becoming passé. There were other reasons such as failed product launches and the failure of DEC to foresee industry trends. DEC was essentially stuck in the past as a corporation, and it was in a downward spiral.

Anxiety was in the air at my workplace. Since late 1995, downsizing was occurring on a weekly basis and a few employees would be let go each time. The employees would be offered severance packages and access to outplacement services. By now, I had seen a few of my close colleagues leave and this was painful. Working for years alongside many of these colleagues, empathy was felt for their plight. Workplace rumors abounded. The workplace had now become one of anxiety and fear. Many of the support reps had families and this new insecurity about their future added to the existing job stress.

Following each instance of layoffs, the remaining members of the support center would breathe a sigh of relief that they had been spared. We kept hoping that the downsizing was finally over. Unfortunately, the downsizing continued. I was called into my manager's office in the spring of 1996. I knew that this would not be constructive as I was rarely called in. My manager would often leave us to manage ourselves. It was now my turn and a severance package was placed before me!

This came as a shock to me. I had never experienced being let go in any of my previous positions. I would always be the one to decide to leave a position. There was no choice in the matter. The offer was explained to me and all that was necessary was my signature. The only choice available to me was not to accept the severance package. However, this would cause me not to receive any future monies from DEC. As with most people with bills to pay, there was no choice in the matter. The offer was accepted and signed while at the same meeting. The severance package would compensate me for a few months and access to an outplacement agency was provided. This agency would hold regular sessions with downsized DEC employees and provide guidance for our futures. We would also be able to tap into their database and network of services.

I had not updated my resume in many years and the outplacement agency provided me assistance with this task. This was also the era when home computers were not commonplace and their office facility could be accessed to research job opportunities, write my resume, and discuss career options with them.

I recall one of the meetings where my interests were shared with an outplacement counselor. The counselor asked specific questions to determine the type of employment that would best suit me. It is simple to assume that I would just seek a similar position to my most recent one. The counselor attempted to determine if this type of employment was even suitable for me. Would I perhaps enjoy doing other work in life? The questions asked were primarily non-technical and focused on the kind of things I derived enjoyment from. There was also a personality test as part of the meeting.

My woodworking hobby was brought up with the outplacement counselor and how I enjoyed creating tangible objects. My woodworking journey of recent years was discussed as well as the joy it brought to my life. We also talked about my technical career and the demand for my skills. The counselor was curious about the passion I demonstrated whenever woodworking was discussed. We talked about my thoughts of being involved in a woodworking business. He seemed to support this direction and asked me to give it further thought. Perhaps after twenty years of working in the computer field, I was ready to make a career change? It was a fairly productive meeting and I left with many unanswered questions to ponder over.

After a few sessions at the outplacement company, the shock of being downsized was slowly overcome. I also began to regain my confidence and felt more secure in speaking of my future. By now, my resume was up to date although I was not ready to seek new employment. Thought was given to the many changes experienced in the computer industry over the past twenty years. Having witnessed first hand over two decades of evolution in both hardware and software; it felt as if I was on a technological treadmill. I was in a constant state of attempting to keep up with the latest technology.

Changes in the computer industry were occurring fairly rapidly in this era. As a testament to this, a large company like DEC could not keep up as they missed some industry forecasts and got it wrong. My former employer, Data General, was also on the decline. Data General did, however make the decision to embrace UNIX early on; this kept them solvent for a few years. Computer systems were rapidly shrinking in size and low-cost home computers were becoming commonplace by now. Complex minicomputers were becoming very standardized and had simply evolved into server boxes. Other large computer makers such as SUN Computers were experiencing a plateau, where sales had peaked and were on the decline. It was a strange era since computers had become very ubiquitous by now, yet a whole chunk of industry jobs were disappearing. Reliability of computers had vastly increased over a twenty year period and large pools of support individuals were no longer required.

All these thoughts raced through my mind, and questions were raised as to whether I wanted to continue in this industry. Solace was found in woodworking where technological change was very minimal. The same tried and true woodworking techniques used to create furniture today were used many decades ago. Machines were slowly introduced to the woodworking industry, where many of these machines had been developed over a half-century earlier.

With this in mind, the decision was made to hold off on seeking new employment and instead to pursue woodworking. With all the new free time available to me, I could make a concerted effort to advance my skills and perhaps create some marketable products. More time was then spent in my workshop working on box designs.

Late in 1996, I joined a local arts and crafts guild. After attending a few meetings, I entertained the thought of setting up a booth at one of their upcoming craft exhibitions. This motivated me to create additional jewelry boxes. However, the experience at this first craft exhibition was an eye-opener. A table was set up to display my assortment of boxes. The boxes were my first generation boxes and simple in design. People stopped by but next to no sales were made.

Almost diagonally across from me was another box maker and his sales were brisk. I was curious as to why people would stop by my booth and then move to his booth to purchase. What caused these people not to purchase my work? My boxes were appealing and priced right or so I thought. After a while, I walked over to talk to this other craftsman about box-making in general and inquire to his experience. We had a conversation and he decided to come over to my table to have a better look at my work.

Upon inspection, he recommended that I invest in better quality hardware and work on better box designs. He found my boxes to be very ordinary. It was discovered that this craftsman had been creating boxes and selling them through the guild show for a number of years. He had a vast amount of box-making experience. His advice was taken in stride and I returned to my workshop. Over the next few months, I challenged myself to create new, more complex box designs.

The jewelry box designs now being developed were far more complex than my earlier models. I loved to challenge myself and would continually add new features to the boxes. Through research, it was found that clients preferred larger jewelry boxes. The boxes were now becoming larger wider and deeper. More levels were also added to the interior of the boxes. Some levels had sliding trays and the hinge system currently used was completely replaced with quadrant hinges. The boxes would no longer have dangling chains. Essentially upping my game, my new work was radically different from the boxes entered at that earlier guild show!

This new challenge and mission kept my mind off my loss of employment. Convincing myself to spend time one year at woodworking, it could then be determined if I wanted to return to a computer career. Changes in the computer industry were fast- paced. Excluding myself from these changes for a few years could spell the end of my career. The thought was that a one-year break would not create too much of a dent in my employment record.

A First Business

"The entrepreneur always searches for change, responds to it, and exploits it as an opportunity"

Peter Drucker

OVER THE NEXT YEAR from 1996 to 1997, my focus was completely on woodworking. A new business **White Mountain Design** was registered and I began to read up on business. Advertising for my jewelry boxes was also begun. E-commerce was in its infancy in this period and I connected with a more established Internet site that marketed locally crafted goods.

This site provided me access to sales in Ottawa, Ontario, my home market. In this period, I was confident of my woodworking skills. With the education previously acquired and the practical application in my workshop; I had confidence in my jewelry box designs. A finishing process had also been perfected for the jewelry boxes. As well, the interiors were now lined with velvet. A technique to create small, moveable tray dividers was also implemented. The boxes had by now become larger with multiple levels. A new box would often be designed and shown to a small circle of people to determine their reaction. If the design was popular, it was then offered as a product. In the late 1996 and early 1997 timeframe, cigar humidors had begun to be very popular. As a non-smoker with little interest in cigars, the potential market could still be seen.

Very soon, it became obvious that a cigar humidor could essentially be similar in construction to a jewelry box. The interior would, however, be different. Research began on humidor articles and techniques on how to build them. The process by which a humidor keeps cigars fresh was interesting. It was necessary to have a certain amount of moisture within the box to maintain the cigars and to keep them from drying out. The interior was typically made of Spanish cedar and well sealed from the ambient air outside.

I considered designing such a box utilizing the same general dimensions as my jewelry boxes. After researching humidor sizes, the jewelry box dimensions were found to be perfect. The challenge was to create a tightly sealed cedar interior. This was accomplished soon enough. The humidors had raised lips of Spanish cedar that interlocked with rabbeted cedar panels in the upper lid. Without going into too much detail, the design was successful. It was also necessary to have a humidifier unit in the humidor that would generate humidity and maintain moisture equilibrium. These humidifiers were sourced and I was able to get wholesale pricing. A hygrometer was also added to the inner lid to indicate the humidity level in the humidor. Initial feedback received from my circle of friends and acquaintances was very positive. The humidor designs were placed for sale on the other company's E-commerce site referred to earlier.

Since digital photography was in its infancy in this period, photos at the web site were crude and of low resolution. Surprisingly, inquiries were received for both jewelry boxes and humidors. In early 1997, a jewelry box with a lower drawer was also offered. This particular design involved considerable work since the construction of the box case had to have a slot and rails to accept a drawer. Processes were developed where multiple components for multiple boxes were created at a time. This allowed me to produce the boxes in a much shorter timeframe.

The business was beginning to get recognition. A new logo and business cards were designed and were handed out at every opportunity. The humidor market was rapidly expanding and a small cigar store had set up shop in a trendy part of town. After discussions with the proprietor, we agreed that I would sell my humidors at his business. He offered a variety of different humidor designs where my particular design would fit a certain niche and price point.

Exposure was also gained through two large food and wine events held over the course of 1997. My humidors would be featured at these events. Considerable interest in the humidors was received during and after the show, with a few sales resulting. Due to the popularity of humidors and the fact that I was in the right place at the right time with this product; brisk sales were enjoyed for the next while. Humidor sales soon overcame jewelry box sales.

A wide variety of both jewelry boxes and humidors were now offered. The boxes were typically of dark woods or light woods. Maple would be the choice for a lighter box and mahogany, cherry or walnut for a darker version. I decided not to apply stain to any of my products. The wood would attain a natural patina and color on its own. Cherry naturally darkens with age and walnut actually becomes lighter in color with age. Tops in highly figured woods such as birds' eye maple or tiger maple were also offered. The corner joinery used was miter joints with reinforcing splines.

Three-level black cherry jewelry box with sliding trays (1997)

The corner joinery reinforcement was hidden by utilizing this approach. The aesthetic of the boxes was clean and very contemporary looking. Also available as an option on the jewelry boxes was a brass lock inset into the front of the box. Overall, the boxes were popular and demand slowly increased. My sales were local at this time and my jewelry boxes and humidors also became available through two other retail outlets. In the summer of 1997, I decided to create my own web site and research began on how to perform this.

A FIRST BUSINESS 81

With my considerable computer software background, I thought it should not be difficult. Around this time, Microsoft began to offer a primitive web site software development package, **Front Page**. This software was purchased and time was invested in developing a web site for **White Mountain Design**.

Within two months a web site was ready. By today's standards, this web site was very crude and appeared to be in a little disarray. There were no defined web site standards in 1997, so a web site developer did not need to follow a specific layout. The web site browsers at the time were also limited to Internet Explorer and Netscape. Compatibility was a problem and often a web site that worked well in IE appeared as a total mess in Netscape. It was a struggle to get the web site to render well, but I managed to accomplish this through trial and error. Also, web site coding was largely accomplished directly in HTML (HyperText Markup Language) which had not been standardized between browser vendors. I have to say it was both an exciting and frustrating time to be developing a web site. The saving grace was that expectations were low and most other web sites of the era also appeared to be haphazardly put together.

My new web site had important components such as images, prices, descriptions and how to order. The decision to develop and create this web site was primarily made to maintain control of the web site. I found it necessary to have frequent updates performed to my product listings at the earlier E-commerce site. Each update was time-consuming and was charged back to me. With my own web site, I could instantly make my own updates free of charge. A domain name was also acquired at this time. With everything ready, the new web site was hosted at a startup internet service provider in my area. The ISP helped considerably with the process of loading and setting up the web site on their server. The web site was up and running by mid-1997. I began to investigate search engine optimization around this time and defined keywords for the web site to rank well when popular keyword strings were entered.

SEO optimization was also in its infancy and most web site developers would learn as they went along. There was considerable web site trial and error at the time as documented processes were still being written.

In my search for the keywords and strings set up for SEO, it was found that my site ranked well. Keywords such as "humidors", "jewelry boxes" were popular and so these words became my focus. The result of this effort was exciting. Inquiries from all over the USA and Canada were soon received as well as receiving inquiries from Europe. People were interested in my jewelry boxes and humidors. The pricing covered my material costs and provided me with a decent profit margin. The labor necessary to create each box could only be partially determined since they were being created in multiples. I felt well compensated with the pricing set at the web site.

However, an interesting phenomenon occurred. When a price was decided on, the currency was not defined. Since most of the web site inquiries originated from the US, the pricing was assumed to be in US dollars. In the 1997 timeframe, the currency exchange rate of US to Canadian dollars was close to 35%. A Canadian dollar was valued at 62c or so in US currency. The end result is that with each sale in the USA, my profit margin increased by 35%. I could not believe this was occurring. It was in my best interest to retain US pricing and also mentioned this explicitly at the web site. In light of this, the pricing was kept reasonable. The vast majority of inquiries and sales were to originate from the US. This sheer coincidence and profit windfall motivated me to pursue box making as a business.

Within weeks, I was overwhelmed with new orders. Since this was now my full-time work it was easy to keep up. As an early adopter of E-commerce, this experience made me a firm believer in selling over the Internet. Working feverishly to keep up with orders, rugged packaging was designed to ship the orders in. The fragile nature of the jewelry boxes and humidors would necessitate highly padded boxes. I researched packing and shipping as well as seeking advice from a local UPS vendor.

A FIRST BUSINESS

The decision was made to ship UPS as they would handle the processing of customs paperwork. My clients would pay for shipping from Canada over and above the price of the jewelry box or humidor.

Sales were brisk and my boxes were being shipped across North America as well as orders to countries in Europe. Clients were largely satisfied with their purchases. Occasionally, a few clients were asked for sales testimonials. It was discovered that sales testimonials were excellent for acquiring future sales. People like to hear from other folks that had a good experience with a product. In some of the feedback received, two clients mentioned that they found my prices too low. It was interesting to hear this from clients!

The advice was taken to heart and the prices were slowly increased. The orders received were considerable and I convinced myself that if higher prices impacted sales then the prices could always be reduced. The plan did not fail and the orders were reduced to a manageable level. I was pleasantly surprised at the compensation being received for every jewelry box sold. The currency exchange rate would add an additional 35% profit margin to every sale. As a home-based business, this had become a success. Soon I was beginning to feel cramped in my basement workshop. The process of creating multiples of these boxes generated considerable dust. Although there was a rudimentary dust collection system in place, it was not nearly as sufficient as necessary. It was a fairly regular occurrence to sweep the walls of dust as my dust collector could not keep up. It was debated whether to expand the workshop into another part of the basement, but this was decided against as it would impact the accessibility of the basement. Another part of the basement was already being used as a finishing area.

In light of this, I was at a crossroad. Should the business be expanded to a larger, dedicated facility or continue to struggle with issues of dust and limited space in my basement?

I continued with the status quo for a while longer. In the meantime, attempts were made to devise methods of work that would require less space and generate less dust. The experience acquired in this process was invaluable. Within a one year period, my products were being exported across North America as well as some countries in Europe.

A web site was developed and my reputation as a quality jewelry box and humidor maker was growing. My three level jewelry box design with a drawer was extremely popular and is still produced today, almost twenty years later.

A completed mahogany jewelry box with two levels of sliding trays and lower drawer. Front handles are wenge (1998).

A Return To School

"Learning never exhausts the mind"

Leonardo da Vinci

A DIFFERENT DIRECTION OCCURED in late 1997. An employment counselor approached me about the availability of computer skills training. This was government sponsored training to provide new computer skills to people that had involuntarily left the workforce for a one-year minimum. This training opportunity was somewhat interesting to me. Since leaving both college and university, I had programmed computers, but only at a basic level. I was able to write code and understand software programs which enabled me to diagnose problems.

The new training program at CompuSkills Institute would be to learn a new set of programming skills where I would graduate as a UNIX Application Developer. The programming language taught in the program was C/C++. This language was extremely popular in this era and people familiar with C/C++ programming were in demand. I was aware of this prior to discussing this opportunity with my employment counselor. The training would provide me with new UNIX Application Development and C/C++ skills enabling me to restart my computer career as a programmer. This would also be a new direction in my computer career.

The opportunity was very tempting. I mulled over the decision for a few days and decided to accept the training offer. The training program began in the fall of 1997. The training would be over a period of two semesters where I would graduate in early summer of 1998. In light of this programming training, a temporary pause would need to be placed on my woodworking business. This was the best approach to allow me to focus on the training. I began to get excited about this new programming training and reread a few programming books in my possession. This would give me a head start on the initial classes.

My class had a group of students from different backgrounds. The other students were in a similar situation as mine; we had involuntarily left the workforce for at least one year. The reason for selecting students who had been unemployed for one year was to prevent people from leaving their jobs for this expensive training. Although the government administered the training, a computer studies institute, CompuSkills, provided it.

The classes were intense and the training was condensed. It was critical to not miss any of the classes. Classes were typically held in the morning and we performed programming exercises in the afternoon. The exercises would reinforce what we had learned that day. We were also given assignments to be completed before the start of each class. The opportunity to reinvent myself as a computer programmer stoked a fire in me. Once again, I began to enjoy working with computers. Along with a year-long absence from computers, my disillusionment with the computer industry had now vanished.

Most of my computer employment until this time had been in support roles. Throughout my career, I was constantly diagnosing and troubleshooting hardware and software problems. In the latter part of my career, my role was to diagnose operating system and software application problems. I would constantly be exposed to the negative aspect of computers, the failed software and hardware. This resulted in not performing anything creative with computers. After some introspection, it dawned on me that this was perhaps the cause of my disillusionment with the computer industry. By programming computers for a living, perhaps something creative was being performed?

I would be writing computer programs. I recalled the period a few months earlier while developing my web site. Although the software was frustrating to use, a sense of accomplishment overcame me as the web site evolved.

I got along well with the other students in the course and developed a sense of camaraderie with a few of them. We would share stories of our previous careers and our lives. We were all in a similar situation and were making an effort to reinvent our careers. Some of the students had little prior experience with computers whereas a few of us had a previous computer career. We were now all in the training program to become UNIX Application Developers.

Each day brought a new lecture where we learned new commands and programming techniques. The exercises involved creating short programs that implemented the commands we had learned. We were expected to write the code and to provide data input to the short programs. The code was then compiled and programming errors would be diagnosed and fixed. The correct data output would validate the computer code. Days turned into weeks and after a few months the fall semester had ended. By the end of the semester, we had succeeded in programming a fairly complex program implementing much of what we had learned. A sense of accomplishment was felt and I was anxious for the next semester to begin.

Over the winter break, a return to woodworking occurred and time was spent creating the components for some of the more popular jewelry boxes. The boxes could then be quickly assembled when orders were received. The compensation from the sale of these boxes would help considerably with my living expenses. Over the past year and a half, I had transitioned from a well paying computer career to being self-employed. The only compensation now received was through sales of my jewelry boxes and humidors. My expenses and overhead were also factors in achieving a profit. The second semester began and more learning occurred. The students had all returned except for two individuals. I overheard that they had offers of employment and opted out of the training.

The remaining students were excited to begin since we would graduate as UNIX Application Developers in a few short months. We began in early January and would complete the training program in late May. The second semester would be more intensive than the first. As well, we were expected to complete a project. The instructor had already decided upon the project. We would each complete a similar project, where each student would produce a different implementation of the project. The project was to write a Virtual UNIX emulator in C/C++. We would need to implement all the commands and routines we had learned over the course of two semesters. Library routines would also be created and used. The program would run on a Windows platform and emulate a series of UNIX commands. The emulator could list a directory; search a directory, copy files, move files and display files.

The project was disclosed to us early in the second semester so we could begin to work on it in our free time. The lectures were as exciting as the lectures of the first semester, and we learned new subject material each time. Occasionally, I would struggle with how to implement a part of the project only to learn about it in an upcoming lecture. The application of the software also reinforced the knowledge.

During this period, I dramatically curtailed the orders processed at my business since it was important for me to succeed in this training. Some clients were willing to wait for many months to receive their order where others simply cancelled. Advertising for new orders was also stopped while in this training program. After completing the program, the option was available of seeking employment with my new programming diploma. I could also return to making boxes at my business. These options gave me peace of mind, although I would definitely be seeking programming employment. Work also progressed on the Virtual UNIX program. We were asked to have the program emulate a basic set of UNIX commands, the core commands to list, search, copy, move and display files. It was optional to enhance the program with additional commands. The program involved structured programming in the C/C++ language.

A RETURN TO SCHOOL

Structured programming lends itself well to modular programming. The program becomes a collection of modules that are designed to work together. As an enhancement, I decided to add a few command line options to some of the commands emulated in the program. These options would add functionality to certain commands. For example, ls -l would display a list of files with more detail than without the -l option. I also added "mkdir" (make directory) functionality. The command "pwd" was also added to be able to display the current working directory. The project was successfully completed and it was graded very well.

Virtual UNIX V3.0

Project Leader: Norman Pirollo

Copyright 1998
All Rights Reserved

Completed CompuSkills Virtual UNIX emulator project, Spring 1998

In spring 1998, I graduated from the CompuSkills UNIX Application Developer program. It was somewhat of a relief to graduate as the training became quite intensive towards the end. We had pressure to complete our projects as well as absorbing the final lectures.

Company recruiters also visited the training institute and interviewed a few of us. We would select which company recruiter to meet with; this was dependant on the type of employment we were seeking. My decision was for a position involving programming. I met with two company recruiters but was unsuccessful in getting employment at that time. Since my new skills were in demand, immediate employment was not much of a concern. When combined with my previous computer experience, there were no concerns about finding employment. With all this in mind, I left the training institute and pondered once again over my future. For peace of mind, a few months were allocated to finding the right employment. Employment would be sought which hopefully utilized my recently acquired training. Summer was in the air and I had no worries!

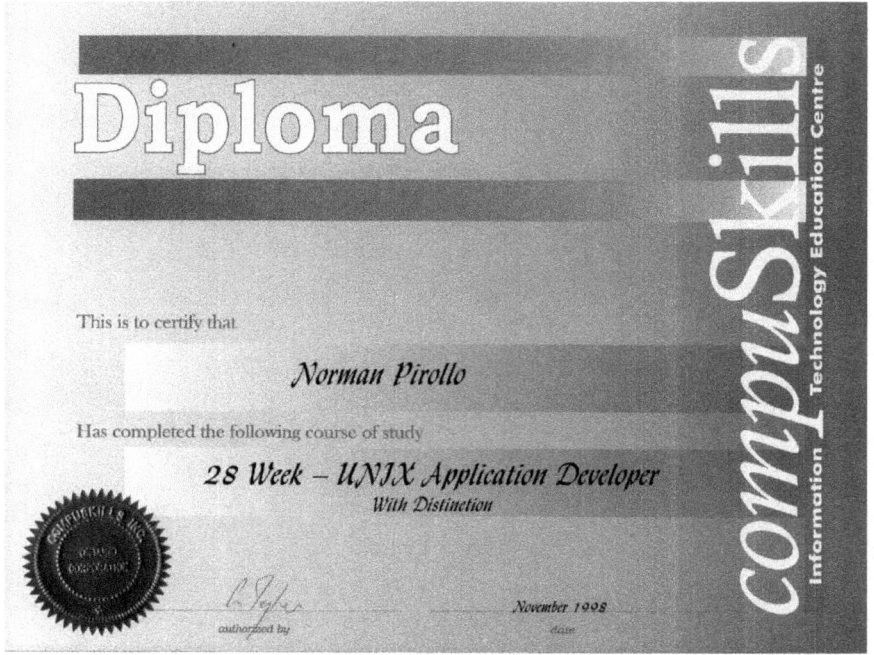

CompuSkills UNIX Application Developer Diploma, received 1998

A Summer Project

"Every project has challenges, and every project has its rewards"

Stephen Schwartz

WHILE SEEKING EMPLOYMENT an idea for an interesting project was hatched. I had read about a software package that was designed for training purposes. Companies would use this software to create training packages. The software would be used to create interactive training. The idea was that this would be an excellent method to deliver woodworking training. Computers could be combined with woodworking. The trend at this time was moving towards online training. This particular software was quite powerful and designed with the user in mind. Inquiries were made about acquiring this software. The cost of the software and commercial license was quite high. It was critical to make an informed decision before moving ahead with this project.

The radical, new idea of offering woodworking training over the Internet grew on me over the next few weeks. With further inquiries about the software package, it was discovered that there was a local vendor to provide me a demonstration of the software. Upon meeting with the vendor, I was shown how they use this software. This vendor actually developed training packages using the training software and I left quite impressed.

Shortly afterwards, the training development software was purchased along with a commercial license to use it. The commercial license would allow me to develop a training package and both market and distribute it. Research began on the best approach to develop the online woodworking training. It was decided to offer it as a comprehensive course. Having been taught woodworking using a traditional approach, wood basics are taught, then hand tool basics and then machines and power tools. Joinery was taught as its own subject. Training modules for each of these topics could be developed and written. Further research into creating interactive training led me to the topic of storyboarding. This is where the training is detailed and broken down into modules. The storyboarding process was followed in the creation of the woodworking training.

The scope of the project was very large and since the training was comprehensive, many woodworking topics would need to be covered. Utilizing the storyboarding approach, a list of ordered modules and lessons was drawn up. The lessons within the modules were then developed. The interactive training slowly came together using this sequential process. Developing the woodworking training using any other method would have been daunting.

Purchasing the expensive training development software package gave me the motivation to go forward and complete this project. Soon, storyboarding of the training had begun with work on the initial modules and lessons. The training would be a combination of text and images, with one image on every page. The training could be accessed on a computer and was set up as a book. At the end of each lesson and module, there would be a series of multiple-choice questions. I found the quiz element of the training to be an excellent method of reinforcing what was just learned. As the days and weeks went by, additional modules and lessons were completed. Much of the photography used in the training would need to be created as well as using some stock photography **(creative license images)**. The combination of text, images, and interactive questions was quite powerful.

A SUMMER PROJECT

Students were able to restart a lesson if they did not perform well in the question session. My excitement gradually grew about this woodworking training and the fact that it could be distributed on a CDROM. The woodworking course project continued over the next days and weeks. Each day, text for each of the lessons within a module was written. To make sense of it all and to maintain my sanity, I allowed myself a few days to complete each lesson. This approach continually motivated me as the lessons and modules would build on one another. The approach worked well, although some lessons took longer than planned while other lessons were created in less time. A criterion necessary to overcome was the limited data size of a CDROM since the complete course would need to fit on a single CD.

This was accomplished through the careful juggling of lessons and modules and by combining other lessons. Technical support was also available to me for the software package used to create the training. I tapped into this on more than one occasion. The local vendor also helped considerably in addressing any issues experienced in the development process.

I recall working many hours each day over the summer of 1998 to complete this woodworking training. The lessons and modules were coming together and the project was finally completed later that summer. After some deliberation, I decided to label the woodworking training simply as a **Woodworking Course**. After some exhaustive testing and fixing of software issues and bugs, the new Woodworking Course CDROM course was ready to be marketed. In my market research, it was found that there was no other similar woodworking training on the market. A new niche had been created.

Later that summer, it was decided to begin some test marketing. Additions were made to my existing web site which described the course in detail. A photo of the CDROM was also inserted at its own web page and a reasonable price was set for the course. The SEO (Search Engine Optimization) of my web site was also tweaked to have additional keywords and "meta tags" in place that would rank my site higher on "woodworking course" Internet searches.

While developing this woodworking training, I continued to seek employment. My resume was sent out to several companies. One interested company did contact me early in September 1998. The company developed and distributed database applications along with search engine software. An interview was arranged for a few days later. The interview was a success and within a day I had an offer of employment. The position was to provide technical support of their search engine software. The work was interesting to me as it would utilize much of the C/C++ training I had recently pursued. The company, **Fulcrum Technologies**, wrote their software using these two languages. The job would be locally based at their Ottawa company headquarters.

In the meantime, orders for my new Woodworking Course CDROM began trickling in. After shipping a few of the CD's and waiting a period of time, my fiancée and I decided to contact a few of the students (clients). We would ask if they enjoyed the Woodworking Course and if they had any issues with it. There was some anxiety in asking these questions since the Woodworking Course CDROM delivery mechanism was very new and revolutionary. I had no idea of how it would be received by the public. The few clients we contacted were overwhelmingly positive about it; they were excited to learn about woodworking while at their computer. At the time, a booklet of projects and notes was also included with the course purchase. This part of the woodworking training encouraged students to work on simple projects.

Over the next few weeks, the woodworking course package was fine tuned and optimized for quicker access. The editing portion of the development was also ongoing, with small corrections performed where necessary. Overall, the Woodworking Course CD was a success. I have been marketing this product for over fourteen years. In this period, two lessons and a completely new module on Veneering have been added. The photography was also updated a few years later as the quality of digital images improved.

A recent photo (2012) of the updated Woodworking Course DVD.

Three years after completing development of the Woodworking Course, a leading US Technical Training Institution, **CIE**, approached me. They wanted to offer my course as part of their woodworking curriculum. We agreed on pricing for volume purchases and the woodworking course was soon offered at their web site for students to purchase and learn woodworking. The institute has been a regular client of mine for a number of years.

A New Phase

"The first step toward change is awareness. The second step is acceptance"

Nathaniel Branden

THE LAST MONTHS OF 1998 WERE a productive time in my life. Within the year, I had completed an intensive computer-training program and graduated as a computer programmer. This new knowledge along with over twenty years of experience in the computer industry provided me with a new outlook on computer industry employment. A new position was begun at **Fulcrum Technologies** in early fall of 1998 where I was assigned to work with a mentor over a two week period. The new company was much smaller than my previous employer and the employees were like family to each other. The Ottawa headquarters included both a software development center and a small support center. My role was search engine support where I would often interface with the software developers. We communicated any new software bugs directly back to them and were then provided with software fixes. The search engine software supported was used by software integration companies as part of their own software applications. My role was also to field support calls that the software integrators had. Attempts were made at reproducing problems and either provide the clients with a solution or communicate the problem back to the developers.

As part of a four-member team, we performed similar support roles. A few members in the team had been there for years and were considered senior members. At the beginning of my employment, I would often ask them for advice and assistance. The search engine software was not terribly exciting to support but the skills acquired in my recent computer training were being utilized. After a hectic first few weeks, I settled into the position. There would be no further training necessary; instead it was to be on the job training. Many of the support calls received were similar to one another. Other calls were more complex where it was necessary to reproduce the problems. Once a problem was successfully reproduced, it would be far simpler to diagnose and provide a fix. If the problem was not reproducible or there was no available fix, the problem would be escalated to the developers. The developers were located in another part of the building.

Since the search engine software was fairly static with occasional updates, my support job could easily be performed without much anxiety or stress. In other words, there were very few surprises in the job. After consultation with a senior member, it was my role to decide if a problem should be escalated. A sense of camaraderie was established with the group of people I worked with. We would often have lunch together and enjoyed extracurricular activities after work.

In light of this, more time was available to me to spend at my woodworking. I felt it was important to work at White Mountain Design and maintain it as a viable business. The additional earnings from sales of jewelry boxes would help a great deal with my living expenses. Orders resumed at **White Mountain Design** and a few evenings were spent each week working on jewelry box and humidor orders. The box design developed over a year earlier had become my main product. This design was versatile in that it could be configured in different woods or configured as a humidor. A new model of both a jewelry box and humidor was also offered featuring exotic wood banding. The banding framed the carcase and was typically wenge, a black ebony-like wood.

Woodworking Course CD sales were also increasing where a sale was made every day or every other day. When combined with the jewelry box and humidor orders, overall sales were quite good. I was constantly seeking new methods to market my products. Magazine advertising was a component of my advertising with ads running in two woodworking magazines on a monthly basis. The ROI (Return on Investment) of these ads was quite good. Occasionally, I would experiment with the ad and modify the ad copy to determine if it had a better response. One version of an ad would be running in one magazine, while another version ran in the other. This allowed me to determine which ad was more successful. Of course, this was also dependant on the size of the subscriber base of each of the magazines.

The Internet was by now becoming established as an E-commerce medium. The sophistication of browser software was increasing on a monthly basis. A cottage industry of SEO performance companies had sprung up to help small companies such as mine to acquire higher ranking in browser search results. With my background in software, this was a challenge that could be easily tackled. After all, I had developed and written my own web site and was already experimenting with meta tags and keywords.

People were slowly becoming more comfortable with ordering over the Internet. E-commerce payment methods were in their infancy where each transaction was processed manually. Bank costs for this were high and reduced my profit margin for each sale. Since people like to be comfortable with a transaction, each transaction had to be processed through bank credit cards. Working with major credit cards and established banks made people secure with their E-commerce orders.

The year 1998 became 1999 and both my job and business were advancing well. I invested time at my woodworking and experimented with new box-making techniques. Time was also spent creating other small projects and at improving my workshop area. The workshop by this time was beginning to feel cluttered and a dose of creativity was necessary to find efficient methods of storing tools and reduce clutter.

I made more use of wall space for storage as well as storing little-used tools outside the workshop. Slowly, it became obvious that a much larger workshop was necessary in which to conduct my business. Woodworking shops tend to grow into the tools you own. The many tools and machines purchased over the past two year period would need to somehow fit in the workshop. Dust continued to be a problem and I made it a point to clean the shop more often. This would reduce the dust accumulation and help me to maintain both my health and sanity. As much as my love of woodworking, the side effect of dust has never appealed to me. Dusty environments do not sit well with me!

The next few months of 1999 were without any surprises. Everything was going according to plan. Sales increased month over month and my orders were being fulfilled. A routine was developed where work would be performed on different parts of the box orders each evening, much like an assembly line. As the summer of 1999 approached, boredom set in with my software support job as it was not what I had expected. An attempt was made to understand if it was the job or my return to the computer industry that was the issue. Perhaps the monotony of the work was causing me to lose interest? Or the satisfaction received from woodworking was impacting my day job?

The thought of transitioning to woodworking on a full-time basis crossed my mind more than once. After some preliminary financial projections, it was determined that I could support myself at a reduced income. My marketing could be ramped up by processing more jewelry box and humidor orders. The US exchange rate continued to be extremely favorable to the Canadian dollar and so my margin per order was high. The limiting factor was my current workshop size. More orders could not be processed in this location; it was simply not designed to function as a business space. A larger workshop would need to be rented or leased if I decided to expand the woodworking business. Of course, this would increase my business overhead and be somewhat financially self-defeating. In early fall of 1999, my manager asked to meet with me. I was given the bad news that my position was being eliminated!

There would be a severance package offered to me and as typical in these situations, there was little choice in the matter. The release forms were signed and I left the company within the hour. In reality, this news was not terribly upsetting to me. I was torn between this employment and striking out on my own and so the decision was conveniently made for me. Over the next few days, serious thought was given to the future direction I would like to follow. The severance package combined with my business income would be sufficient to provide me with many months of earnings. In light of this, there was no rush to make a decision. The larger decision was whether I wanted to even remain employed in the computer industry. My dilemma involved the recent programming diploma that had been obtained. By walking away from the computer industry, this effort would be wasted. With much hand wringing, the decision was made to not seek further employment. After being downsized for a second time, it was increasingly clear that I could not focus on a new job. It was best for me to take a break and spend time at woodworking instead.

This recent downsizing also provided me the motivation to consider self-employment as a viable option for my future. Over the next few months, considerable time was invested in weighing my options by performing research into the cost of scaling up my business. A larger space was necessary to be able to process more orders. A greater investment in machinery would also be necessary although I could get by with my current machinery for a while. The largest expense would be renting a workshop space and the overhead associated with operating the space. Utilities, business taxes, advertising, heating, and lighting would all factor in as overhead expenses. An increase in orders would be necessary to offset the additional overhead. I asked myself if all this made sense. Was it worth the risk of leaving regularly paying employment to take these risks? Being unemployed helped in the decision. I had given myself a financial buffer of a year's income from which to draw while deciding. This would complete my twenty third year of employment in the computer industry. Should I continue with this career or reinvent myself at a completely new career?

A New Millennium

"Sometimes it's the smallest decisions that can change your life forever"

Keri Russell

THE YEAR 2000 BROUGHT much introspection and decisions with it. Early in the year, after lengthy discussion and agreement with my spouse Linda Chenard, the decision was made to pursue woodworking instead of returning to the workforce. The decision was not an easy one as it meant giving up on the computer industry for employment. The issue of workshop space was at the forefront. My current location, the basement area of our home, could not be expanded for many reasons. Noise, dust, space and even zoning restrictions would all be factors influencing my decision.

Linda and I discussed the options available to me. We would need to either move to a property with a dedicated workshop or remain where we were and a workshop space rented instead. We were fortunate that the city we live in has a rural component that is actually part of the city. With this in mind, we visited a few properties for sale in the outlying rural area. A rural property with a workshop would provide me with considerable space for expansion. Noise and dust would not be an issue. Rural zoning would also be accommodating to a woodworking type of business. Early in the year 2000 we sought out properties through a real estate company.

We were assigned a real estate agent and every few days a call would arrive and off we went to visit a property for sale. One of the criteria was the need for an existing large outbuilding on the property. The outbuilding should be in good condition and amenable to a woodworking shop. The age of the house was also a consideration along with any improvements done to it. Along with our agent, we searched far and wide. Some properties were closer whereas others were too distant from the city core. This search proved to be more difficult than anticipated. Whenever we found a home we liked, the outbuilding was either in poor condition or completely not suitable for woodworking. If we found an excellent outbuilding, the home would have issues. We never seemed to find a good pairing of home and outbuilding. A few of the outbuildings had been used for farm animals and, therefore, had concrete stalls installed. This would be difficult to undo. Other outbuildings were in general disrepair and primarily used for storage. Many of the homes we visited had issues with water potability or the location of the house was poor. The layout of a few homes was also not appealing to us where the interior was dated. Some homes were on busy roads and although conducive to business, presented a danger if we decided to raise a family.

After this experience, we were somewhat discouraged with the process of purchasing an existing property. The real estate agent continued to search on our behalf while we considered other options. After what we had seen, the temptation to remain where we currently lived was greater now. It was obvious that we needed to move, however. Our home was listed for sale and offers to purchase came in shortly thereafter. Within weeks, we had sold the home. It became more critical for us to find a new home. Since the home was sold, I soon could no longer continue woodworking in my present workshop. We had two months to prepare for a move. The urgency of finding another home was high. Another option available to us was to have a new home constructed on a larger property and have an outbuilding built at the same time. This would allow me to set up a workshop and continue my business. In this transition period, I would stop receiving all orders for jewelry boxes and humidors.

With this option in mind, we visited a few rural homebuilders and discussed our needs with them. We liked one of the builder's homes, they were modular in nature, and factory built and then moved on site. However, the criteria of an adjacent or separate workshop could not be worked out. Another option was to have a large workshop built as part of the home instead of a separate workshop. This option allowed for tapping into the heating, cooling and power of the home, reducing the construction and operating costs considerably. We continued discussions with another builder or two and finally found a homebuilder that would construct a home for us with a fairly large adjacent workshop.

The appeal of a new home was great. We would not need to update the home for many years. Aside from a mortgage, since the home was new, we could live in it relatively cost-free for many years. We could have it built to our specifications and layout. This last builder specialized in this type of rural construction. He designed a home with our criteria in mind and a few weeks later we would agree on the design. It was decided that the new workshop would be a few times (6x) larger than my current workshop. It was to be located adjacent to the home, behind the garage, as a separate facility. It would have its own power panel and noise isolation would be factored in. The ceilings would be higher than average and a large amount of lighting would be installed. It also made sense to have the workshop on (2) levels. Machinery could be installed on the lower level with a bench room in the upper level. Both levels would have many large windows to bring in as much ambient light as possible.

The process of building a rural home was somewhat different than simply purchasing a tract home in the city. We would need to purchase the land first, and then have a home built on the property. The builder also had land available in a rural area very close to the city. We selected a property of close to three acres and began to plan the timetable to have the home and adjacent workshop built. Other rural factors also needed to be considered. A well would need to be drilled, the land would need to be partially cleared and utilities would need to be run across the property.

The timetable decided on would provide for a four-month window of building and completing the home. Since one level of the workshop was essentially below ground, water table issues would need to be considered. We instead opted for a higher and drier tract of land on which to build. Since the home would be a few feet above the water table, this would ensure that basement flooding would not be a concern. Sump pumps are also mandatory in rural construction to prevent basement flooding. New construction would also ensure that adequate drainage was installed around the perimeter of the home. This was all fairly new to my wife and I and it was quite a learning experience. We took it all in stride and enjoyed the home building journey.

The homebuilder also gave us the option of renting us a home while our own home was being constructed. This rental home would be a historic home a few miles away. I wanted to be close to the building site to be able to monitor the construction. Since the homebuilder had other homes to build during that summer, we agreed that I would help to oversee the construction of our home. Not being employed that summer, this worked out well for both of us. With a temporary rental home available for us to move into, the decision was made to pack our possessions and store them away for a few months. I meticulously began to take my machinery apart to be able to move it. Some of the machines that I wanted to upgrade were sold; they would be replaced after moving to the new workshop. The rest of the tools were packed well and treated to avoid rust while in storage. Within a few weeks, arrangements were made with a mover and the bulk of the contents of the home were placed in storage.

We moved into the rental home and the process of having our new house built began shortly afterwards. The orientation and location of the house on the property were decided on. This was to be the very first step. The land was cleared and footings were poured. The layout and size of the home could already be distinguished from observing the footings. Next, the foundation was poured and preparations were made for the main floor to be constructed.

Many of the building steps would occur sequentially, but a few occurred simultaneously. Having a homebuilder or general contractor oversee the construction of a home cannot be emphasized enough. A homebuilder not only designs the house but makes arrangements with all the trades people that work on the construction. The timing of tradespeople became important, as many steps in the construction process could not proceed without completion of the previous step.

Once the foundation had cured, the framing of the house began. We had a dedicated crew of framers assigned to the home and for a period of three to four weeks they would work diligently at framing. This part was very exciting and with each passing day the house would look more complete. Of course, this is not the case since there is so much more to constructing a house. At the very least, the shell of the framed house was encouraging to see.

Framing of new home and workshop, trusses being installed (2000)

Over the next few weeks, the house began to slowly take shape. Some last minute design changes were necessary. For example, room layout and window locations were changed.

I recall the day that the trusses for the roof were being installed and the roof panels installed. On this day, the house began to look like a home. Interior walls were framed and the workshop space began to take shape. I was very pleased with the final size we decided on for the workshop area. It was a nice size and the lower level was a similar size. A set of stairs would join the two levels. The window sizes selected for the workshop were large and brought much ambient light into the workshop area on both levels.

Several contractors were scheduled to work their magic over the next four months. We decided on a combination brick and siding exterior where brick would be on the main level of the two-storey home as well as the workshop walls. The workshop itself extended out from the home a few feet along the back wall to accommodate its large area. There were very few surprises and the build went well.

The final stage of construction involved the installation of ducting, electrical wiring and the furnace. I decided on a more practical location for outlets in the workshop area, they would be at the four-foot height. This was to accommodate benches against the wall. It was also arranged to have (2) 220V circuits installed. These would power both a new table saw and industrial jointer. I had not purchased any additional machinery yet, but these power requirements are fairly standard. Since this time, additional 220v circuits have been added to the workshop.

Bricks were laid early in September of 2000 and the siding and soffits completed. The roof had been shingled a few weeks earlier. The interior of the home was now drywalled and painted and floors had been laid. Aside from overseeing things, I participated in some aspects of the build. I installed the hardwood floors on the main level of my workshop and built landings from the workshop doors to the garage area. Noise isolation of the workshop area was also one of the criteria of the house build. With some expert advice, we decided on building a double wall between the home and workshop. This double wall would have noise deadening insulation installed as well as acoustic channeling with two layers of drywall.

Considerable thought was also placed into keeping dust from the workshop areas away from the home. Since the workshop utilized heating and cooling ducting from the home, air returns would be a problem. Air returns would bring dust-laden air from the workshop back to the furnace. This was not acceptable. Instead, I designed a passive air return. Forced air ducting would be channeled to the workshop but air would be returned to the furnace instead through a filtered slot in the adjoining wall to the home. The positive pressure of forced air in the workshop areas would eventually pass through this filter system and maintain a pressure balance or equilibrium. As well, the furnace would draw air through this filter area to accelerate with the balancing effect. I am glad to report that the system has worked exceptionally well over the years.

The home was completed in late September 2000 and we moved into the home in that timeframe. I was able to move some of my tools into the workshop but would need assistance with the machinery. A layout had been long planned for the machines and so every tool and machine had its place. A comprehensive dust collection system was also installed. The dust collection system consisted of pipes and hoses, all 4 inches in diameter. As well, the system was divided between (2) dust collectors. One dust collector would handle a few machines, whereas the second dust collector the other machines. This reduced the load on each of the dust collectors. There is a recommended limit to the length of piping for each collector and having two systems resolved this issue. A series of blast gates was also installed.

Shortly after move-in two additional machines were ordered and delivered. These new machines, a new commercial 3HP cabinet saw and 3HP industrial thickness planer were installed and routed to the dust collectors as well. The new workshop area would soon become a work in progress. I decided to work in the area for a while to better understand optimum bench placement and location of wall cabinets.

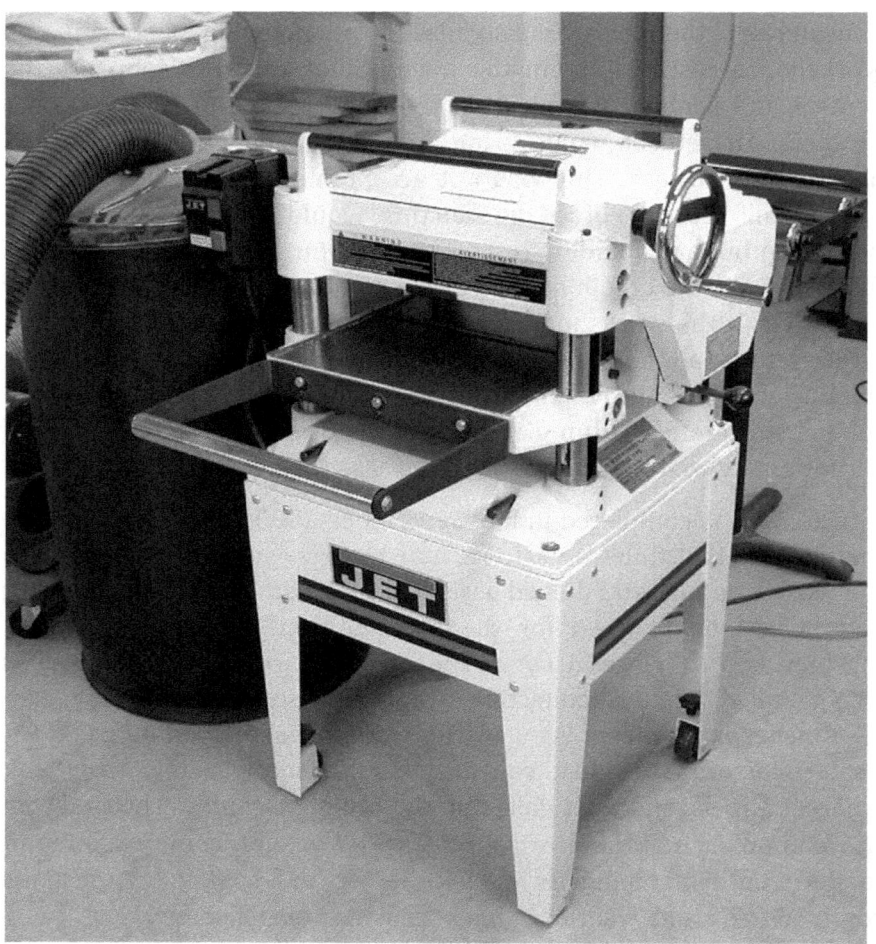

New 15in. 3HP thickness planer with dust collection in lower level of workshop (2001)

The smaller machines such as a 6 in. jointer, 13 in. thickness planer, drill press and band saw were installed along the perimeter of the room. This layout made the most practical sense. The large cabinet saw was placed directly over an I-beam in the center of the upper level. This placement would transfer weight away from the upper floor joists.

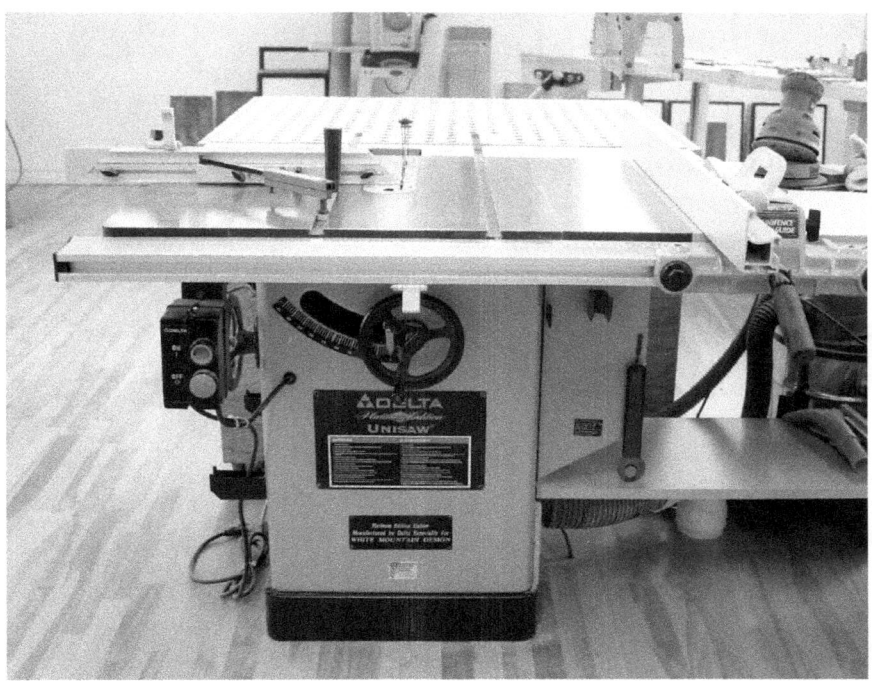

New custom 3HP table saw with dust collection, extension (2001)

There was much to accomplish in the home as is the case with new house construction. Finishing touches continued to be applied to kitchen cabinets and the washrooms of the house. Some exterior work was begun as this was early fall. Grading of the soil around the home was performed. This was a priority since it was important to have the soil sloping away from the home. Eavestroughs were also installed. After deliberation over how to complete the patio area, we decided that I would instead build a deck and begin this project the following spring. Since the patio door was considerably higher than the surrounding soil, it was necessary to build a deck with a platform and stairs. Until this was done, we could not get a final inspection on the home. Most of my free time was invested in setting up the workshop after move-in. I was keen on getting my woodworking business back up and running as soon as possible.

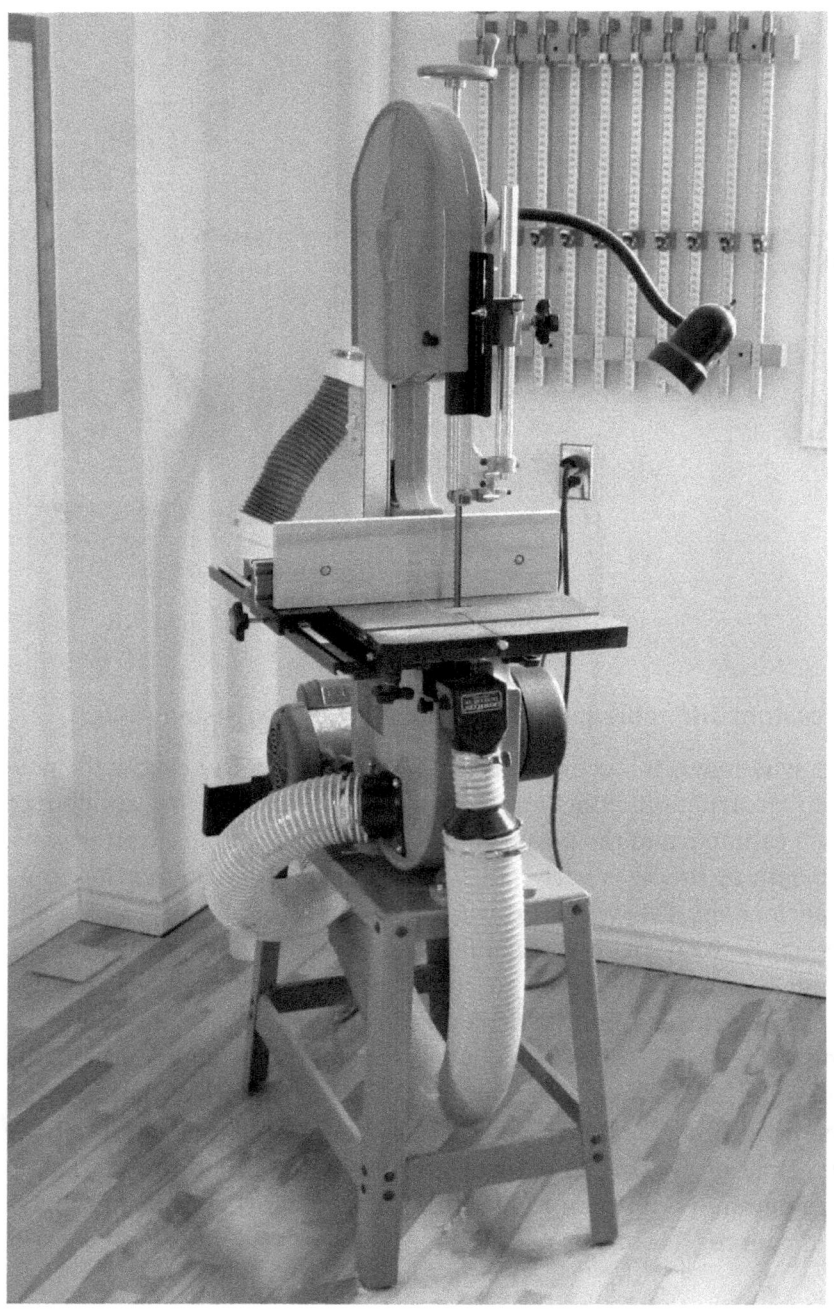

My original band saw with upgraded fence, dust collection (2002)

A Dilemma

"There are three constants in life...change, choice and principles"
Stephen Covey

IN THE EARLY PART of the house construction, a headhunter contacted me. With a focus on completion of the new home, I had no longer been seeking employment. Without the new home and workshop, continuing with my woodworking business was not possible aside from selling copies of my Woodworking Course CD. The head hunter asked about my availability for a job opportunity. The possibility of this was mentioned to him and that I would be rather busy over the next two months. In light of the circumstances, this was my best response rather than say I was not interested. This answer provided me with time to work on the house construction and a decision could be made from there. The head hunter was vague about the position except that it would involve a support role at a large, multinational company.

He mentioned he would get back to me at a later date and I thought nothing more of this. There was no interview planned nor was there further information. The focus continued on house construction and every effort was made to have it proceed smoothly. My spouse and I even went as far as purchasing all the plumbing fixtures for the home and having them delivered to the house. This would save us time later.

As construction proceeded we would make installments on a temporary line of credit we had established. We would also pay the tradespeople as we went along, for both materials and labor. This was the arrangement we had set up with the homebuilder. Before we began construction we purchased the land that the house would reside on. This would be our very first expense. As different parts of the house went up, we would have more bills to pay. Initially, there was an estimate of the cost of building the house. This amount, along with the cost of the land, was to be the final cost for the house.

When the construction was complete, the final amount was exceeded by approximately fifty thousand dollars. This was due to the fact that we had not factored the cost of the land into the equation. We assumed that the land was part of the cost of the home. This misunderstanding was directly due to having purchased two new tract type houses in the past. The price of each tract home always included land. This is not the case when building your own custom home on a rural property. Land is a separate purchase and never part of the cost of building a house.

We would need to scramble to find this money. Bills were outstanding and we had to begin repaying the line of credit we were borrowing against. The proceeds of the sale of the previous home had already been applied to the cost of the new home. I had also tapped into my savings. We had no choice but to increase the mortgage of our new home. This was unfortunate since we had already budgeted a certain amount per month for the home mortgage. We could marginally afford the mortgage amount along with other bills such as property taxes and utilities. With the increased mortgage, we now had a financial dilemma.

I began to give thought to returning to work, even at a part-time position. This would allow us to afford the larger mortgage payments. With a part-time position, I could continue to work at my woodworking business. In light of this mortgage dilemma, there was an even greater motivation to get my new workshop ready.

A DILEMMA

I recalled the conversation with the headhunter a couple of months earlier and decided to contact him. Not having heard back, it was assumed the position he was referring to had been filled. Contacting him would also let him know to look for other employment opportunities. With nothing to lose I contacted him. Interestingly, he recalled the conversation we had months earlier. I inquired about the support position with the multinational firm and he said he would look into it as he had also not heard back. Within a day, he called and mentioned the position was still available. He also had more details about the position.

The position would essentially be in a support role for the UNIX OS and networking applications. The computer company was one of the largest in the world and the position was based in my home city of Ottawa. The most interesting detail was that I would only need to complete a three-day a week shift of twelve hours each day. My ears perked up when this was mentioned. Until this time, I had not been seeking employment and decided instead on full-time self-employment. My new workshop was taking shape and would offer more than sufficient work space for my business. My business could be expanded and I could hopefully survive at it.

The dilemma Linda and I faced was the large discrepancy in the amount of mortgage we would need. We had built this new home and workshop with my self-employment in mind. Over the past year, we had convinced ourselves that this was my best move. I could focus on my business and hopefully be successful at it. We also had additional costs that had not been factored into the original estimate. These were the costs of the move and setting up the new home interior. We decided to slowly replace furniture with some of the furniture I would be making.

I recall being torn in the decision to pursue employment. After mulling the job position over and discussing with the headhunter; he made arrangements for an interview. He interviewed me over the phone and the next step would be to interview with the multinational computer company. I had never experienced such indecision in my mind; ultimately convincing myself that there would be nothing to lose by being interviewed.

The company name was also disclosed at this time. Hewlett-Packard was a giant in the computer industry. Travelling to another city for the interview, a meeting was arranged with both a human resource representative and the hiring manager. We discussed my background and my skill set. The position was explained in more detail. The three-day a week part was very appealing to me. It was convenient to be able to work twelve-hour shifts of the shortened work week. The only other caveat to the position was that two of the days would be weekend days. This was cause for concern for me. It would mean that I would rarely have free weekends aside from dedicated vacation time. On a positive note, four days of each week were available to pursue my business. The compensation was average but the short work week was more interesting at this time. It was also mentioned that the position was a second level support position. My work would be in the background diagnosing escalated cases and assisting front line support reps. The interview ended with mention that I would need to give it thought as well as consulting with my spouse.

A few days later and after discussions with my spouse, a decision was arrived at. Due to the precarious financial situation we were now in; I would need to work at a job regardless. Although originally envisioning part-time employment, this job offer was similar in style to a part-time position. Most of the week was available to operate my woodworking business and then work three days at HP from Friday through Sunday. With my extensive UNIX background, it would not be difficult to adapt to this support role. There would be some initial formal training and mentoring included. The team was based in Atlanta, Georgia where I was a remote member of the group. My direct manager would be local and the technical manager would be based in Atlanta. It was a complicated arrangement, but it made sense at the time, and so I joined Hewlett-Packard in a UNIX Support role. As work progressed on the completion of our new home and workshop, travel to Montreal occurred to begin a few mentoring sessions. The initial mentoring session introduced me to the HP reporting and research systems as well as providing me a glimpse of the HP implementation of UNIX.

Follow-on mentoring allowed me to work with my peers who performed a similar job to mine. Within weeks, I was sent to formal training courses. The training was over a period of two weeks. A short six weeks later and I was ready to begin my new position working solo. This arrangement would be the best of both worlds for me. Being employed now, a financial cushion was available to draw from. The free time available during the week could be dedicated to establishing my woodworking business and setting up my new workshop. It was a busy time, as these new directions in my life would need to be juggled. The new home also involved much of my time. This was a period of my life where I worked the hardest. Wanting to be successful at the new job; considerable time would need to be devoted to learning about **HP-UX** (HP version of UNIX). Since positions like this do not come available very often, I would work at this new job for two to three years until I was financially back on my feet. The woodworking business would be able to support me after this time. A concerted effort at expanding my business would also need to take place.

The remainder of 2000 was quite busy with so many changes in my life occurring simultaneously. The HP job demands began to settle down as training was acquired. The training was in another city and this meant being away for a period of two weeks while my home was in the final stages of completion. We were moving in a few days after my return from training. In the first three weeks of the new position, I worked alongside another support representative. This was all accomplished over the phone via three-way conferencing between a client and two HP UNIX Support reps. I slowly felt more comfortable with the position and was able to snag a small HP-UX system for my home office. This allowed me to experiment with HP-UX and also be able to reproduce client problems. This also allowed me to experiment with new versions of HP-UX and configure networking applications. When we designed our new home, a dedicated office on the ground floor of the home was planned. This was an enclosed room with a door. The office was to be where the woodworking business was managed. This demonstrates the extent of the commitment I had to a full-time woodworking business.

A New Direction

"If you do not change direction, you may end up where you are heading"

Lao Tzu

THE YEAR 2000 SOON ENDED and 2001 began. I had settled in with my support position at Hewlett-Packard. The team I was a member of worked well together and we would assist each other when diagnosing more difficult problems. My role in the team was second level support and my involvement included escalations or issues that could not be resolved by front line support staff. This provided more of a challenge to me. My salary helped considerably with the unforeseen expenses we had in setting up our new home and equipping my workshop. An investment in larger, industrial style machinery was made in recent months including larger capacity dust collectors, a cabinet saw, and the larger capacity thickness planer. An investment was also made in some smaller hand and layout tools.

After settling in to the new workshop, orders for jewelry boxes and humidors had resumed. This was a priority for me as it was necessary to demonstrate business continuity. There were already many months that had lapsed since I stopped accepting new orders. This can be detrimental to the credibility of a business.

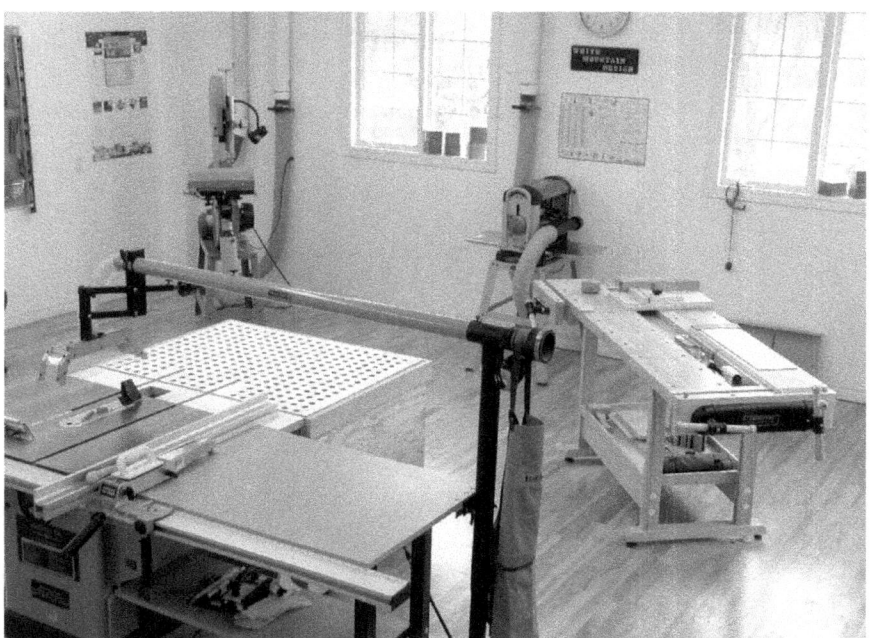

The new workshop showing band saw, table saw, workbench and dust collection system (2003)

In the spring of 2001, thought was given to alternative products to create and market through White Mountain Design. Although jewelry box orders maintained the same level as previous years, the humidor component of the business had significantly dropped off. There had been many other humidor makers that began to market their products over the past years and competition became fierce. As is the case when a product rises quickly in popularity, everyone jumps on board and seeks market share. Therefore, prices of humidors were dropping and to compound the problem, imported humidors were slowly overtaking the market.

It would be increasingly difficult to compete with these newer, much lower price points. Jewelry box makers were far fewer as there was much more complexity in creating jewelry boxes in my style. Without the need to make more humidors, my woodworking business had extra capacity available for other products. Designing a new product had now become more appealing to me.

The criteria for a new product would be consumer demand and the size and the complexity of making it. With the experience gained from producing jewelry boxes, it became obvious that size was critical. If the product was too large, shipping methods and costs would be a challenge. My jewelry box design was as large as I would like to create a product and be able to ship it within North America and Europe. Enjoyment would also need to be derived in making a new product; it had to provide some challenge in its design and functionality. Rather than seek a mass-produced product, I sought something that would target a smaller niche. The needs of the niche were hopefully not currently being addressed!

After considerable market research, I considered making wooden hand planes. The hand plane market was growing and the typical hand planes on the market at this time were metal-bodied hand planes. Renowned author and woodworker James Krenov wrote one of the textbooks from a college woodworking course. Krenov romanticized woodworking in his series of books. His attention to detail was inspirational. The journey of creating was just as important to him as the final piece of furniture. Wood selection and grain orientation were very important in his furniture designs. He also made his own hand tools, especially wood-bodied hand planes. Reading and re-reading his book made me curious as to why he would make his own tools when so many high quality tools already existed in the woodworking marketplace.

James Krenov explained the philosophy behind his hand made tools and detailed the process he followed to create hand planes. The book had and continues to have widespread appeal among woodworkers. Shortly after rereading his book **The Fine Art of Cabinetmaking**, an attempt was made at creating my own wooden hand plane design.

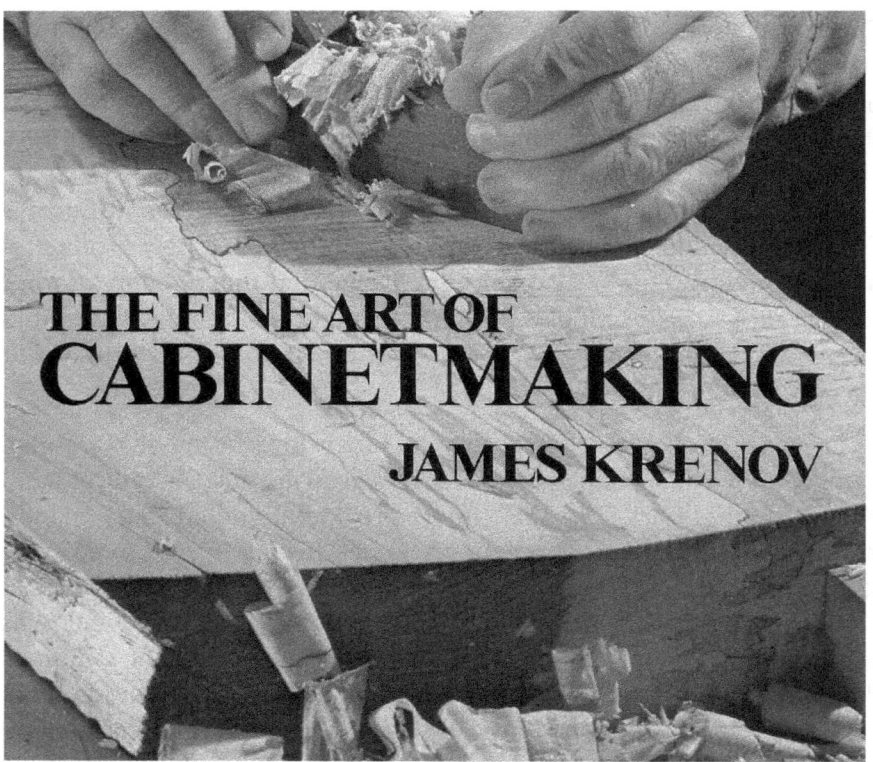

Over the next few weeks, I experimented with the process of creating a wood-bodied hand plane. Work also began on one such hand plane, although it was quite crude. I wanted to determine if this was feasible as a product. Work continued with both research and experiments and I was successful at creating a wooden hand plane. At the time, there was only one reputable supplier of irons for wood-bodied hand planes. **Ron Hock** was contacted to discuss volume pricing. His plane irons were specifically designed for wood-bodied hand planes and were very thick.

The added thickness absorbed the considerable force of thrusting the plane forward. The irons were sold with cap irons that both reinforced the main iron and served as a chip breaker. By following the process James Krenov used to create this type of hand plane and reading up on other plane maker's processes, I began to feel at ease with the production of hand planes.

The hand planes were created as a series of components. Each component would be created in multiples where one set of plane components was created each day. This also ensured that the hand plane components were identical and interchangeable. This was the same process developed for my jewelry box production and it served me well. After creating a few basic wood-bodied hand planes, I wanted to distinguish my design from the same, tired looking hand plane design in existence for many decades. A hand plane with a contemporary, organically shaped aesthetic was then designed and tested. This style of hand plane proved to be successful in my marketing. The type of hand plane I focused on was a **smoother** as this was by far the most popular type and size of hand plane. A traditional, square-bodied version of the "smoother" was also designed and marketed

A contemporary shaped smoother hand plane, introduced in 2001.

Once the design of this model was perfected, I proceeded to design two other styles of hand planes. The next model would be a longer **jointer** model. The plane body was made square on this model since a rounded body did not look and feel right. Experiments were also performed with different woods. The soles of wood-bodied hand planes need to be made of wear resistant wood, preferably with natural lubrication. **Goncalo Alves** was chosen for the soles of my hand planes. Goncalo Alves is a dense tropical wood with a natural, slippery surface. The wood used in the bodies was rift-sawn European Beech. Beech is an excellent wood to work with; it has fine grain and can be shaped without much effort. Imported European Beech was used which is more stable than its North American counterpart. Other components of the hand planes were made from dense woods such as cocobolo.

The long square-bodied jointer plane, introduced later in 2001.

Each of the hand planes had a Ron Hock iron assembly fitted; the planes were then individually tuned and tested. The mouth opening on my series of hand planes was fairly narrow to ensure thin, fluffy shavings would be created during hand planing. A narrow mouth opening also reduced the issue of tearout, where divots of wood are torn from the surface being planed.

Tearout can be detrimental when hand planing surfaces of boards. When it occurs, the whole surface will need to be hand planed down to a new level a fraction of an inch lower. The hand planes were finished using a traditional hand-applied blonde shellac finish. The shellac finish ensured that the wood body would not yellow over time. Shellac finishes are natural, solvent-free and completely repairable. The next step would be to begin marketing this new series of hand planes. Pages were set up at my new updated **White Mountain Toolworks** web site for each style of hand plane. Both the White Mountain Design and White Mountain Toolworks web sites were combined, and the **woodenplanes.com** domain acquired to link to the hand planes. The pages included descriptions, detailed images and prices. I was keen to determine the market appeal of this new series of hand planes. A press release describing these new hand planes was issued. Since investing most of 2001 in the development of these hand planes, inquiries began a few weeks later and a few hand plane orders resulted.

The Business Of Woodworking

"So little done, so much to do"

Cecil Rhodes

AS THE MONTHS PASSED my workshop layout began to appear much improved. My main workbench was located in a well-lit area near a window. I also began to build a second much larger, sturdier workbench. It is fairly important that workbenches be stable and their mass and weight help considerably in this task. Large wood components were used to add weight and ensure the workbench was rigid. Different types of workbenches and optimal locations for such components as vises, tail vises and dog hole placement were also researched. This new bench, once completed, would be located in another area of the upper level. After some deliberation, it was decided to do away with a dedicated tail vise. Instead, a system of planing boards was designed which would plug into round dog holes. The planing board system would keep a board from sliding forward while the surface was being hand planed. The workbench was constructed from dimensioned wood available at any home center. The bench surface would consist of two laminated sheets of high quality Baltic birch plywood. I decided on this simple approach to make the workbench both simple to repair and also to be taken apart and reassembled if necessary. The large pieces of dimensioned pine were held together with lag bolts, washers, and nuts.

A large vise was also fitted to the front of the workbench. The vise had maple faces attached to the jaws to prevent marring of clamped wood surfaces. The lower part of the workbench had a large tray installed to be able to hold tools and small parts. Dog hole placement was performed following established standards. I then created a planing board system to fit into these dog holes. The new workbench surface was over five feet long and a few inches deeper than three feet. This size was considerably larger than my existing small benches. The small benches had been designed to fit into my former small workshop. The new, large workbench surface area would allow me to handle large furniture-sized pieces of wood.

New workbench with front vise and sliding board jack (2002)

Wall cabinets were also designed and built for the workshop. I originally had shelving installed but soon realized that dust settles on everything resting on the shelves. This is not very good for tools as it draws moisture in. The wall cabinets would instead contain my hand tools. Over the course of 2002, I built and installed a total of four wall cabinets. With the workshop coming together nicely, I was able to focus once again on making jewelry boxes.

A system of creating multiples of these jewelry boxes was devised using experience gained in my former workshop. I would make up to twenty boxes at a time using this system. Making one jewelry box from beginning to end and then starting another would otherwise take months. By doing it in multiples, all the components for each box could be produced in stages. All the box sides, top, bottoms, sliding compartments and drawer components were created in batches and on separate days.

Mass producing jewelry boxes in multiples, with different wood combinations, tops and handles (2002)

My computer work also occupied my time for a part of the week. Over the summer, I studied towards HP-UX Certification and successfully passed the exam later in the summer of 2002.

There would be two to three weeks per year of additional formal training where I would need to travel. Whenever this occurred, my business ground to a halt. It was all manageable, however, and the combination of shortened work week and business days worked well together. It was a rewarding time as I was living my dream. I had a new workshop, a new home with acreage, a growing part-time business and secure employment.

HP-UX Operating System Certification received the summer of 2002

Even if my job ended I could continue with the woodworking business. Of course, with this attitude, this would never happen! Dust issues of my former workshop were also addressed in this new, much larger workshop. The twin dust collection systems were very powerful and could easily handle dust and chips from any of the machines. Since dust had become my arch enemy, a focus was on techniques to minimize dust creation. In fall of 2002, I read about a fairly new machine called a downdraft table. Downdraft tables had been used in commercial applications and some woodworkers had begun to make their own.

The downdraft table was used as a sanding station and had a built-in vacuum system to draw air through the table surface using an array of holes. There were different variations of these downdraft tables and they were typically small. The concept of such a table was very appealing to me since considerable time was spent sanding as part of the finishing process. Research was performed on how they worked and components were assembled to begin to build one. Since it would be a fairly large unit in both area and height, I decided to create the downdraft table design so it would also function as a table saw outfeed table. One of my interests for quite some time was to build an outfeed table for my cabinet saw, but I could not decide on a clean, practical design. Dadoes would be created in the downdraft table surface to accept the sliding miter attachments of the table saw. As a design criterion, the downdraft table had to be the exact height of the table saw surfaces.

After acquiring a surplus furnace blower motor and enclosed fan along with the wood necessary to build the downdraft table, I set out to build the unit. Using a design made earlier on paper, assembly of the unit began. The blower motor was fitted into a sealed compartment and a system of large filters was set up. The blower would draw dust-laden air through holes in the table surface and force it through these filters. To prevent the dual pleated filters from collapsing, they were doubled up. The electrical system was installed along with a mechanical timer. Boring hundreds of holes in the table surface was the most tedious part of the build. A process was devised to be able to accomplish this while maintaining my sanity!

To clean the lower compartments and filters, the table top was made removable. Once a year, the blower area is disassembled and the motor and fan bearings are lubricated. This downdraft table design has been in use for thirteen years and it works just as it did when new. I am very glad to have built this downdraft table since it removes copious amounts of airborne dust in my workshop. Often, the unit is left running for a few minutes to have it act as a whole shop filter. Since this time dust collection has also been added to my portable sander.

When the downdraft table and portable sander are used together, there is virtually no airborne dust generated. I also installed the airborne dust cleaner built for my previous workshop to help with cleaning the air of airborne dust.

Downdraft table with timer doubles as an outfeed table (2002)

Having the dust situation under control was a great encouragement to me. Recalling my former workshop and the need to sweep dust off the walls, I would never work in a woodworking environment like that again. In this period, jewelry box and hand plane orders continued to arrive. The Woodworking Course CD was quite popular and the images in the course would occasionally be updated with higher quality ones. With my new large and bright workshop, improved photography was now possible. My first digital camera was purchased in 2002, a high quality state of the art model. Until this time, I had been borrowing a digital camera, as they were fairly expensive.

THE BUSINESS OF WOODWORKING

The demands of my three-day per week employment and the woodworking business kept me busy throughout 2002. During the year, the hinge mechanism of my jewelry box design was also upgraded. I would now be using thick solid brass stop hinges. These hinges allow the top to hinge back a few degrees past vertical. Until this time, a pair of standard brass hinges was used along with a quadrant hinge in one corner. The quadrant hinge had a built-in stop. It was difficult to accurately install the quadrant hinges however, and I began to tire of the process. The new rear stop hinge could be accurately installed using special templates provided by the hinge maker.

Updated jewelry box design with Brusso stop hinges (2002)

Although the solid brass **Brusso** stop hinges were expensive, the price of the jewelry box demanded the very best quality hardware. The jewelry boxes have since been built using these hinges. During the 2003 period, I had been also reading up on veneering. Veneering would allow me to obtain greater yield from highly figured boards.

Veneer slices could be applied to a dimensionally stable substrate such as Baltic Birch. The nominal thickness of the veneered panels would be slightly thicker than the solid panels currently being used. I researched the veneering process and read two books on the subject.

In all my woodworking education, I had not been introduced to veneering, as it was a fairly advanced subject in woodworking. Another reason for veneering a panel would be to achieve a seamless panel surface. Commercial veneer sheets could be purchased and then fitted to the jewelry box top panels. My own veneers could also be sawn using a band saw. I preferred sawing my own veneers, as they would be thicker, although purchasing commercial veneers would provide greater variety. Experiments began on sawing veneers and creating larger sheets using narrow pieces sawn directly off the band saw. The sheets were then glued to a substrate. It was soon realized that veneer sheets need to be uniformly clamped to a substrate.

I had been using thick plywood substrates with many clamps as cauls to press the veneer to the substrate. This became more impractical as the area of the veneering increased. Since it was only necessary to veneer fixed-sized top panels for my jewelry boxes, I designed and built a mechanical veneer press. The veneer press design has been in existence for decades and the plan originated from a book read on veneering. The veneer press consisted of many threaded rod and nut assemblies along with a series of curved cauls. The curved cauls would apply pressure to two platens, one above and one below the panel being veneered. This system would apply uniform pressure to the veneer sheet on the panel. The underside of each panel was also veneered to create veneer equilibrium so the panel would not cup or warp. Veneered panels were successfully created using this process but it was found that fixed size panels would be a limitation using the setup.

Mechanical veneer press using threaded rods and cauls (2003)

This leads into 2003 and business was doing well. I enjoyed focusing on my job for three days a week and then shifting focus to my business for the other four days. Working every weekend had become part of my life in this third year of employment at HP. My social life was affected however, since I would be working when everyone else had the weekend off. There was no choice but to continue with this schedule. Often, the thought crossed my mind in perhaps two years I could quit the job and move to full-time woodworking. In the meantime, I wanted to pursue veneering as a larger part of my woodworking. The possibilities were endless with veneered panels. Highly figured woods could be sourced and several veneer slices sawn from each board. The application of highly figured woods in my work was enjoyable as it was discovered that clients sought jewelry box lids of figured woods.

I also wanted to make more varieties of figured woods available for my jewelry boxes. After some time, the mechanical veneer press previously built was becoming a chore to use. The torque necessary on each of the many threaded rods was very high and the whole process was slow and tedious. I thought to myself that there had to be a better way.

After some research, it was found that there were vacuum veneer systems that use atmospheric pressure to create pressure. The vacuum system draws air out of a well-sealed poly bag. It was not necessary to evacuate much air from the poly bag, as the atmospheric pressure would soon compensate in providing pressure. The pressure created would be very powerful and uniform across the panel area. Using this method, much larger veneered panels could be created. The poly bags could also shape themselves to curved surfaces. The vacuum system was appealing to me although it was expensive. After some deliberation, I invested in a commercial vacuum veneering system from **VacuPress Corp.** The system had excellent reviews and could handle veneered panels of up to four feet wide and six feet long. There would be components that were not supplied with the system and these would need to be fabricated.

For the better part of 2003, I invested time in setting up the veneering system and experimenting with it. A dedicated platform for the large poly bag was built which soon evolved into a large bench. This platform bench was very similar in construction to the large workbench built the year before. The vacuum press system also needed a platen with a series of channels crossing the surface. This channel system leads to an air hose used to evacuate air from the poly bag; this platen would need to be created. Successful experiments were made on small panels for my jewelry boxes. Multiple veneered panels could also be pressed at once and the panels would remain in the poly bag overnight under vacuum. The vacuum was self-regulating through a vacuum pump unit.

I was considerably encouraged with this new method of veneering and began experimenting with large panels. Using this new vacuum system, a few orders could be fulfilled for extra large jewelry boxes with veneered tops.

Vacuum press set up to press veneered panels overnight (2003)

After a while, I felt completely at ease with the veneering process using this new vacuum press. It was also decided to document and photograph the veneering process using both my earlier mechanical press and the new vacuum press. A new module on veneering was now included in my Woodworking Course CD. To develop this new module, a few flat panels would need to be veneered and the veneering sequences photographed. This became an educational process since the intricate details of veneering would need to be grasped. Soon after completing the course addition, an enclosed display cabinet was built using veneered panels. Large veneered panels would be a component of the frame and panel doors.

For quite some time, I had been following James Krenov style of woodworking. His signature piece of furniture was the standalone cabinet, usually configured as a display cabinet. The James Krenov book, **The Fine Art of Cabinetmaking**, also documents the building of one of his cabinets. This book was used as a basis for one of my own cabinets. After some planning and design, I began to build the cabinet. The build carried over into early 2004.

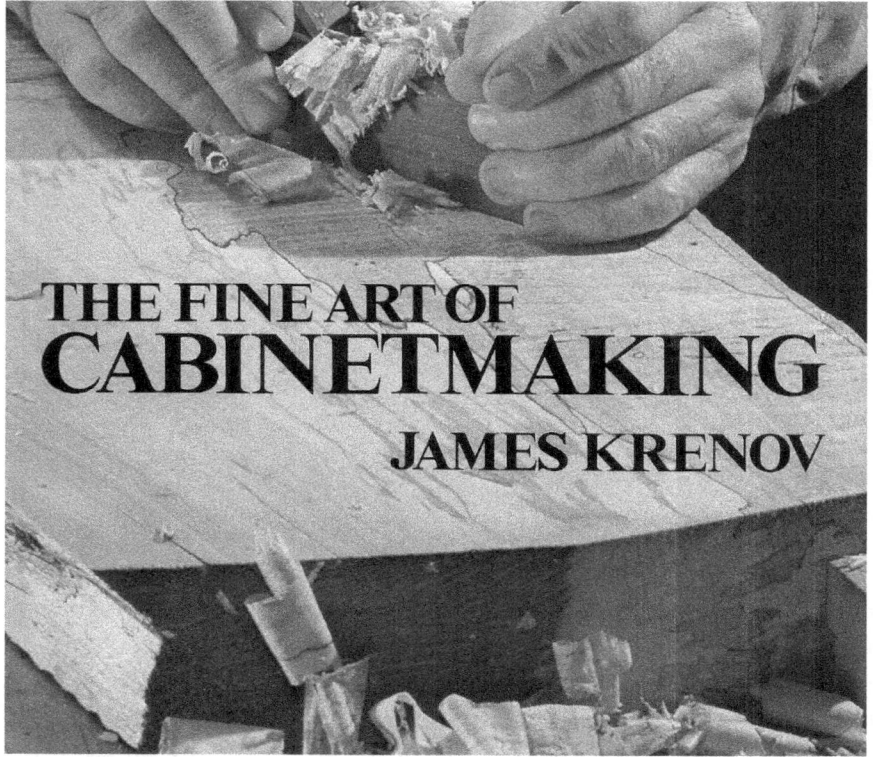

James Krenov seminal book "The Fine Art of Cabinetmaking"

The standalone cabinet was designed to be quite tall and large in dimensions, it was essentially an armoire on legs. While building this cabinet the opportunity came up to read and reread James Krenov philosophy of woodworking. I admired the man greatly and loved how he revered wood and his attention to detail. A large part of his woodworking mantra was to enjoy the process.

Woodworkers today were becoming too preoccupied with quickly building furniture. Machines had been developed and continue to be developed to speed the manufacture of furniture. This mindset had trickled down to the small furniture maker and also down to woodworking enthusiasts. Woodworkers were constantly being bombarded with ads for newer and more efficient machines and tools with complete disregard of the beneficial enjoyment derived in the process.

What James Krenov spoke of was to slow down and focus on wood selection and fine joinery techniques. Krenov also encouraged the use of hand tools, where hand planes would deliver much nicer wood surfaces than sanded surfaces. Sanding of wood was anathema to him as it destroyed the natural surface of the wood. James Krenov worked at a slower pace and never felt rushed. He developed several techniques to build cabinets, his most popular type of furniture. Krenov also introduced small elements and detail into his work where elements such as carved pulls would draw focus to the cabinet. Harmony of the grain orientation was also an important consideration in the design of his furniture.

In light of this, I began to re-think my woodworking processes. Over the years, new methods to speed the making of my products and devising more efficient processes were constantly being developed. These processes involved considerable sanding of components. The methods of work were conducive to a business which was mass-production oriented. Perhaps fewer products could be made where more time could be spent on each unit? All these thoughts became confusing to me as businesses usually seek more efficient processes. Soon it was 2004 and I continued to combine my job and woodworking business. Jewelry box sales had slowed somewhat but would peak around major holiday periods such as Christmas and anniversaries.

My first Krenov-inspired cabinet with veneered doors and sides. Black cherry frame and panel with tiger maple veneered panels (2004)

Hand Tool Redux

"Surround yourself with people you can always learn something from. Always work with people that are better at their craft than you are"

Tony Vincent

IN THE 2003 TIMEFRAME a new woodworking school had recently opened in my area. I looked into the school and found it to be intriguing. The school was founded by a graduate of the College of the Redwoods (California) and followed the philosophy of James Krenov. The curriculum closely followed that of the College of the Redwoods, where James Krenov still taught. James Krenov was instrumental in setting up the original curriculum.

After making inquiries, it was found the cost of each week long course to be somewhat expensive. There were a few courses I was interested in but was not sure if they would benefit me much. Since my woodworking already spanned a ten-year period, I asked myself how much more can be learned? After all, I had studied Cabinetmaking at a local college and starting a thriving woodworking business as well as developing a woodworking course. Would any further education be beneficial to my woodworking? I thought nothing more of it for a few months. After completing my Krenov-inspired standalone cabinet, I began to further appreciate James Krenov's philosophy and methods of work.

Although my jewelry boxes and wood-bodied hand planes with new innovation in the design were successful, I began to feel like a one-trick pony. Building my first standalone cabinet forced me to slow down and focus on the actual build instead of the end product. I find that when woodworkers begin they are excited to create. This makes complete sense since objects beget objects, or success begets success. After many years of woodworking, a typical woodworker will have mastered techniques. The challenge then shifts to design rather than creating. I felt that this was the time for me to develop a new, different approach to woodworking. With my immersion in the James Krenov style of work and these thoughts in mind, my motivation for applying to the new school increased.

My interests were discussed with the woodworking school **Rosewood Studio** coordinator. The initial courses focused on hand tool skills. In the beginning, wood selection and preparation were important topics taught at the school. I assumed my knowledge of this topic was very good at this stage of my woodworking career. It would be strange to return to basic courses after making so much progress at woodworking. I continued to pursue my woodworking business and my work. Further convincing was necessary of whether to invest in these courses.

A few months went by and early in the spring of 2004 I did enroll in a "Craftsmanship" course at this new school. My decision to pursue this course revolved around the fact that the "Rosewood Studio" curriculum was based on the **College of the Redwoods** style of teaching. Since becoming an admirer of James Krenov and his philosophy, I convinced myself that perhaps the exposure to a new style of woodworking would be beneficial. Research into the "College of the Redwoods" curriculum also found it to be refreshing. Since the new school was located in a town not too far from my location in the Ottawa valley, I felt fortunate to be able to travel to courses each day and return home afterwards. The course was held from Monday to Friday of that week. An advantage was that I could attend the course during weekdays, it was only necessary to be away from my job for one day of the week.

I began my first course **Craftsmanship 4** at the school in April 2004. This was to be an Introduction to Veneering, both for flat and curved work. The intensive veneering research performed in the past year helped considerably with this. The setup the school used was very similar to the one used in my own shop. I was most interested in learning how to create curved veneer work and waited in anticipation for the lectures on this topic. While in the course, we created a curved bending form and used it to create curved, laminated panels. The practical learning exercises were excellent at reinforcing what we had learned in the lectures. This would complete the first of two courses I attended that summer.

Prior to beginning the course, each student was provided a list of tools to bring. Although there were hand tools in my workshop, the list requested to bring a No.4 smoother to the course. I was not sure whether to bring my shop-made smoother or a steel-bodied hand plane and so both were packed. A set of chisels was also on the list along with layout and measuring tools. The option was available to purchase any tools not already owned at a store located in the school.

After arriving on the first day of class, introductions were made and the lectures began. I left on that first day realizing there was much to learn and that working strictly with hand tools would be a challenge. In all my years of woodworking, it never dawned on me to work exclusively with hand tools. I thought that hand tool techniques were taught to occasionally work a difficult piece of wood or to fit wood pieces together. This created a new direction in my woodworking.

For the remainder of the course we were taught how to saw veneers and prepare veneers using hand tools. How to effectively use hand planes, how to sharpen and hone the plane irons was taught. Chisels were also covered as chisels would be used in many of the exercises. Veneering processes were discussed over the course of the week. Hand tools which shape wood such as scrapers, chisels and spokeshaves along with tools to cut wood such as handsaws were discussed. In this style of woodworking, hand tools are used to prepare wood surfaces as well as preparing edges.

There was very little machine use aside from the initial cutting of rough planks into sawn veneers. This was the style of James Krenov and College of the Redwoods. I thoroughly enjoyed the course and made a few friends in the process. My initial skepticism had vanished by day two of the course. The approach would teach me to better appreciate wood and work with its characteristics. Grain orientation is a big part of fine furniture construction. Until this time, I had been joining wood to give an aesthetically pleasing appearance but was not following established principles of grain orientation. For example, it is important to select matching grain orientation for the rails and stiles of door. Mixing plain-sawn with rift-sawn or quarter-sawn wood can destroy the harmony and the aesthetic of a piece of furniture. Since my work was predominantly with small jewelry boxes, grain orientation could easily be performed by crosscutting the sides in sequence and then joining the box sides in the same sequence.

With larger furniture, this technique is not possible. To avoid discontinuous graphics, components should be cut from the same boards and in the same grain orientation. The larger a piece of furniture, the more obvious a grain mismatch would appear. This topic was covered at length in the classroom. I absorbed this all and began to feel much closer to wood as a medium. The nuances of wood were also begun to be appreciated; how wood should be revered rather than treat it as a disposable commodity. This philosophy of working with wood would inherently prolong the process of making of furniture but it would be a much finer and higher quality, aesthetically pleasing piece of furniture.

The question arose if this was the style of woodworking I wanted to pursue in my woodworking business. Returning to my workshop after this first week provided me a different outlook of woodworking. Some of what I learned was implemented in the very next piece of furniture built. While at the school, the small store they had set up was visited. Along with an excellent variety of high quality hand tools there was a collection of classic books for sale. Every one of James Krenov books was purchased and the next few weeks were spent reading them from cover to cover.

My excitement grew about this new style of woodworking as it breathed new life into my work. A different outlook of hand tools and their use was upon me. An appreciation developed for slowing down and enjoying the process, rather than simply following the "end justifies the means" approach to woodworking. Within a few weeks I returned to the school for another course. Completing this course continued to steer me in a new direction. It felt as though I was relearning woodworking, but in a completely different light. After each course completion, we had a small ceremony where we were handed a **Certificate of Completion**.

Rosewood Certificate of Completion, Craftsmanship series (2004)

Towards the end of the 2004 summer, I was informed of a course that would be taught by a guest instructor. The school regularly brought in renowned guest instructors to teach more advanced courses. This particular course was called "Advanced Joinery with Yeung Chan". Yeung Chan was an expert in the field. I enrolled in the course and attended class late in August 2004.

Prior to enrolling, the book Yeung Chan had written, **Classic Joints with Power Tools**, was purchased. I enjoy reading up on instructors prior to attending their courses. Yeung Chan excelled at intricate joinery, specifically oriental joinery. He brought a set of hand tools with him as he had travelled from California to teach. He made all the hand tools and they were nicely arranged in a beautiful hand tool chest. It was so exciting and inspiring to see this tool chest in person since there was a photo of the tool chest in his book. The course was intense and we were shown how to create many types of intricate, compound joinery using simple jigs. Most of the joinery was created using a table saw and mortising machines along with specialized jigs we had access to.

Norman Pirollo and Yeung Chan with his intricately built tool chest.

Upon returning from this course, I proceeded to create some of the jigs we used in class. Time was also invested in creating the same joinery we created in class. I wanted to ensure a good understanding of the concepts learned since they were fairly complex.

A series of sample joints was also created to use later when giving demonstrations and to incorporate in my woodworking course. Although the joints appeared complex to make, they were elegant looking. The joints were designed for prominent visual exposure.

Miter jig to create complex joinery in "Advanced Joinery" class. Plans provided by Yeung Chan (2004). I made my own version above, a few weeks after class completion.

My outlook on woodworking had dramatically changed over the course of these few months in 2004. After returning to my workshop and revisiting my methods of work, I aspired to work with hand tools more. Although the dust generation in my shop was under control, my ultimate goal was to work in a dust-free woodworking environment. Hand tools address this well since they only generate wood shavings. A few higher quality hand tools were also purchased over the summer. I have been using these hand tools for over a decade now and they continue to function like new.

After acquiring more hand tools, it was becoming clear that additional storage was necessary. Some wall cabinets were modified to be able to store hand planes and other wall cabinets were designed and created. Additional courses were also pursued at Rosewood Studio over the next three years. The courses were specialized and typically taught by renowned guest instructors.

Three-way miter joints used in the "Advanced Joinery with Yeung Chan" project. Each student would create a stand using this very complex joinery (2004)

More complex joinery created after the "Classic Joints" class (2004).

These were instructors that had successfully established themselves in the field of woodworking, having written books as well as being published in magazine articles. The instructors included Garrett Hack, Craig Vandall Stevens, Yeung Chan and Michael Fortune. Each of these masters specialized in certain aspects of woodworking. They each brought a different approach to woodworking. Typically, their work was excellent and had considerable attention to detail. Garrett Hack and Craig Vandall Stevens are well known for adding elements of detail to their furniture pieces.

Hand plane cabinet to store hand planes and keep dust out (2005)

By attending the courses taught by these master woodworkers, I was better able to understand the hand tool process. The different approaches they each taught would provide me with ideas for creating my own methods of work. The remainder of the courses attended at Rosewood Studio would be over a period of three years. An average of two to three courses and workshops were followed per year. The final course attended in 2007 had to do with Inlay Techniques, taught by Garrett Hack. Always curious about the process to create inlay and after trial and error over the years, I decided to learn this technique from a master.

The course exceeded my expectations and the students created many, different styles of inlay during the exercises. The most complex type of inlay I created was the fan inlay that consisted of multiple segments in the shape of a fan. I also had the opportunity to experiment with shell inlay such as "Mother of Pearl" and "Abalone".

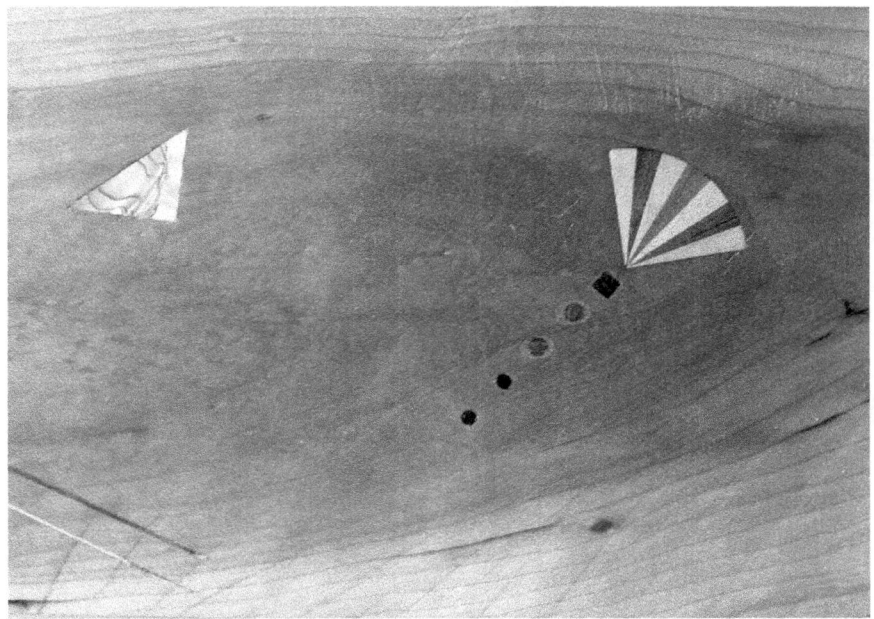

Sample of fan inlay and "Mother of Pearl" inlay in unusual shapes

Craig Vandall Stevens taught another in the series of courses. The course **Hand Skills from East & West** also featured Japanese joinery skills. We were introduced to Japanese hand planes and chisels and how to use them. The course opened my eyes to alternative methods of creating joinery. Japanese hand tools are quite fascinating to use. The Japanese craftsmen worship their tools and invest in very high-quality steel to create them. They are typically all made by hand using century old traditions. My hand tool indoctrination continued through the years 2004 to 2007!

New Work Methods

"The life so short, the craft so long to learn"

Hippocrates

THE PERIOD FROM 2005 THROUGH TO 2007 was a reawakening with new life breathed into my woodworking. Although continuing to make and sell jewelry boxes, my focus shifted to larger pieces of furniture. I was very drawn to standalone cabinets since this was James Krenov's signature style of furniture. Standalone cabinets were also portable and could be disassembled for transport. Figured woods could be selected for components of the cabinet. The cabinets were also functional and a great focal point for a living room or similar area of a home. The challenge of creating beautiful cabinets in the Scandinavian-inspired style of James Krenov, my new woodworking idol, would be rewarding.

Shortly after completing the series of courses at Rosewood Studio in late 2007, I was keen on building a display cabinet that featured many of the skills learned. Unlike my smaller jewelry boxes, there is a considerable investment in wood to build a standalone cabinet. Although a cabinet built on **spec** (speculation) could simply be created with an attempt to sell it, it would be preferable to have a commission from a client for such a cabinet. I began to seek clients who would like to own such a cabinet.

Not long afterwards, I met with a friend and explained my situation. We discussed some options and she mentioned she had always wanted a large jewelry cabinet. Instead of owning a series of smaller jewelry boxes, she preferred a cabinet. A display cabinet configured as a jewelry armoire was immediately envisioned. The cabinet could be outfitted with many drawers and dividers to hold her jewelry. More discussion followed and with her approval, a few initial sketches of the design were drafted and rendered into larger scale drawings. After a follow-on meeting we agreed on the design and the price of the cabinet. Jewelry specific hardware such as revolving solid brass carousels for necklaces would also be installed. The individual drawers were to be lined with velvet and have dividers installed.

The doors were to be frame and panel construction with curly maple panels. Door and drawer pulls were also designed using complementary woods. Blackwood and holly would be used together for a "monochrome" effect. The drawers would have drawer fronts dovetailed into the sides. To hold true to James Krenov style, knife hinges would also be installed to hang the doors to the case. Having already built a cabinet using knife hinges, I felt comfortable with this choice. The cabinet sides, top, bottom, door rails and stiles would be black cherry. Cherry naturally ages over time and would contrast very well with the lighter curly maple door panels. The cabinet stand would also be made from cherry. It was also decided on diamond inlay elements in the cabinet front, which would give it an "art deco" appearance.

Construction began on the jewelry armoire using the new methods of work recently learned. Hand tools were used for a large percentage of the build. Hand planes and scrapers were used on the surfaces of the wood components. Previously, machines would be used for the majority of the work and then hand planes used for fitting. It was surprising at how much I enjoyed the hand tool process. Dovetail joinery of the drawer fronts was also performed by hand using a dovetail jig previously designed. With a total of eight drawers, I hunkered down and created the dovetail joinery at one sitting.

Creating dovetail joinery using my specialized dovetail jig (2007)

Dovetailed drawer fronts in the custom jewelry armoire (2007)

Measuring, layout and marking play a large part in the creation of accurate dovetails. I marked and measured, checked and re-checked a few times to ensure everything was accurate before sawing the dovetails.

The case construction was performed using dowel joinery as per James Krenov. Dowel joinery allowed me to have a top and bottom slightly larger than the depth and width of the case itself. The wider and deeper top and bottom panels could have an edge treatment applied to them; a chamfered edge was decided on. Improvements in the aesthetic of the cabinet could already be seen with the selection of wood made. The components of the cabinet were both rift-sawn and quarter sawn and proper grain matching was performed resulting in harmonious graphics. The cabinet had a calm appearance without a clash of grain. If the wood components had simply been put together without consideration to grain orientation, the cabinet would look odd and unnatural.

Over the next year, a shooting board was also built to be able to trim the end of small boards and components. More hand planes were also acquired, both new and used. Each of the hand planes provided a different functionality. A shoulder plane, a large metal-bodied jointer, and a few other single use planes were purchased. Both a standard angle and low angle block plane were also acquired. The standard angle block plane could also be used as a very small smoother.

My job with HP continued during this period. Similar tasks were being performed as had been for the past five years. As a second level support engineer, my skills would regularly need to be updated. HP offered considerable training in this regard. I was periodically asked to support new software and then went off and learned all about it. If training was necessary, approval was asked for and the course or courses attended.

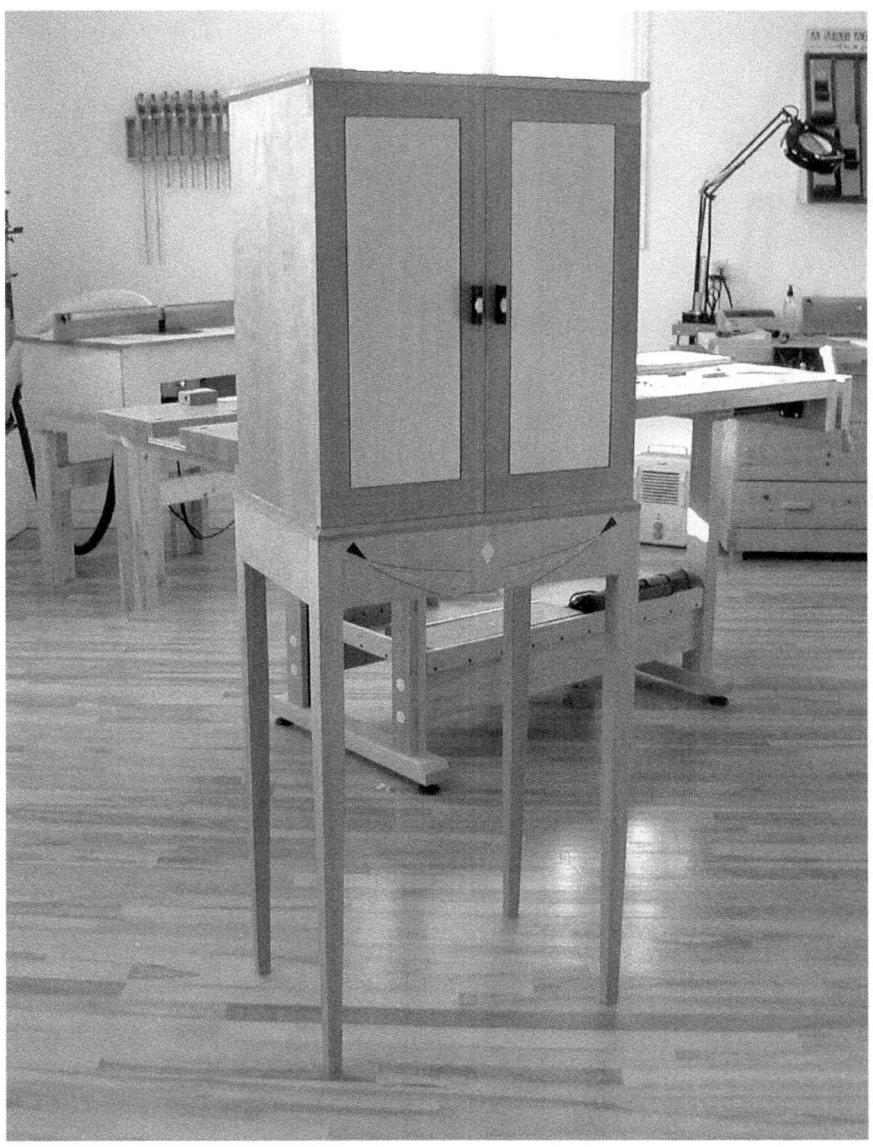

Completed jewelry armoire with tiger maple door panels (2008)

The workshop was now slowly evolving into more of a hand tool workshop. Although all my machinery was kept, the bench areas were enhanced and adapted for hand tool use.

Shooting board used to accurately trim ends of small boards (2007)

Two new dedicated woodworking workbenches were purchased with proper tail vises and front vises. Lower trays were made and installed in each of them. Specialized jigs were also designed to be able to work with small detail saws. Bench hooks would fit over the front edge of a workbench and allow me to cut small pieces of wood precisely at either 45 or 90 degrees. Prior to this, I would think nothing of performing this task on either a table saw or band saw.

With the new hand tool philosophy in mind, methods were sought to perform tasks with hand tools instead of using machines. There would be no setup using hand tools and the operation would be quiet and dust free. Working with hand tools became my new religion!

The surfaces of furniture pieces would be hand planed and scraped instead of sanded. While studying at Rosewood Studio, it was instilled in the students not to use sandpaper. We would not even be allowed to have sandpaper at our benches. Some sanding was allowed between finish coats when applying a finish, but all wood surfaces were only to be hand planed and scraped. This was also the case at College of the Redwoods, where James Krenov taught. It was believed that planed and scraped wood surfaces had greater depth and clarity whereas sanded surfaces were dull. I firmly believed in this approach after seeing and experiencing it myself.

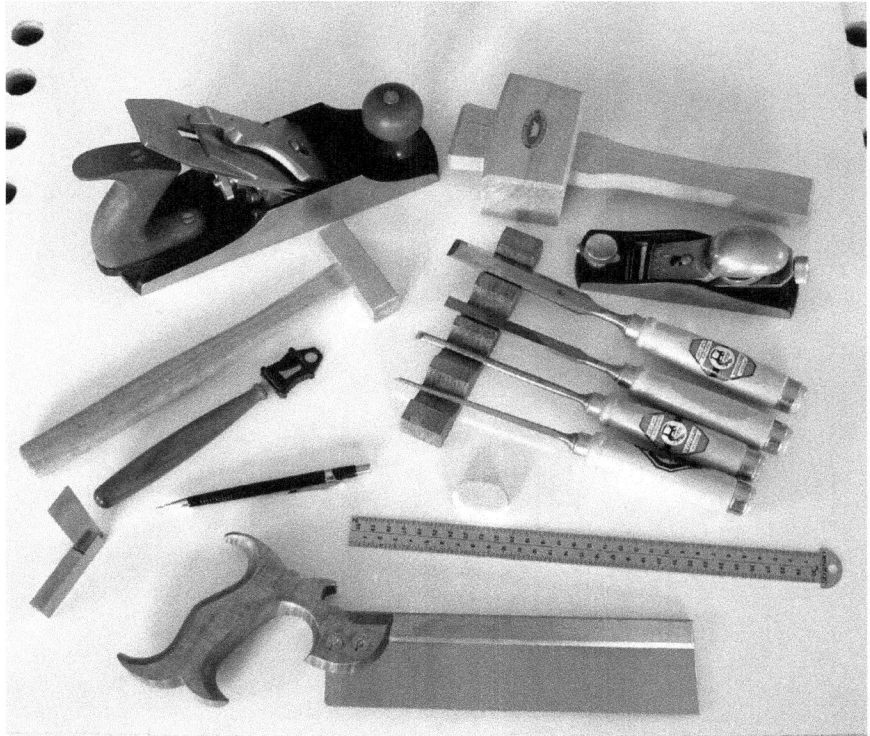

Hand tools used in the creation of dovetail joinery (2007)

The new emphasis on hand tools also encouraged me to remake part of my Woodworking Course CD. Hand tools were featured more prominently along with more text and higher quality images.

Improvements were also made in the jewelry box process by using a shooting board to trim small components. The pieces were more accurately cut using this method. The surfaces of the jewelry boxes were also scraped and hand planed whereas in the past machines and sanding would suffice. These enhancements raised the quality of the jewelry boxes to a new level. With the end of 2007 approaching, thought was given to a new direction. Although continuing to produce jewelry boxes, I felt a larger calling. Creating furniture pieces would satisfy a desire in me to achieve a loftier goal in woodworking.

Hand tool cabinet with clear lexan door panel for chisels and layout tools (2007)

A Fascination With Cabinets

"Focus on the journey, not the destination. Joy is found not in finishing but in doing it"

Greg Anderson

IN LATE 2007 the new focus of standalone cabinets began to excite me. Similar work to that of James Krenov would be created. At the time, I believed there were no better designs for cabinets. After all, James Krenov began the Scandinavian inspired furniture movement.

With this new emphasis on furniture pieces, I decided to make a clean break from **White Mountain Design** and form a new company. Until this time, furniture, jewelry boxes, humidors and hand planes were combined into one web site with categories for each. This was found to be confusing to a client seeking any of my work. After exhaustive research and numerous name combinations, the name **Refined Edge Design** was decided on. The name really appealed to me as it spoke to the refined edges of my furniture. After tossing the name around to a few individuals, the general consensus was that it was a cool name and accurately described my workmanship. The next steps were to register the business name, set up a new web site and populate the site with recently completed furniture pieces. The added expense of hosting another web site was well worth it in my opinion. A new logo would need to be designed along with new business cards and marketing material.

New Refined Edge Design business card (2008)

The new business process was completed early in the year 2008. The business motivated me to devote more of my focus to furniture making. From feedback received, the standalone cabinets I had begun to create were very appealing. The attention to detail, dovetail joinery, inlay and other design elements also fascinated people as this was something rarely seen in mass-produced furniture. Two additional standalone cabinets were designed and built during the year, each one made from different woods. Popular woods were cherry, beech and maple where each of these woods had unique characteristics as well as different densities. Maple is a slightly harder and denser wood than cherry, beech has a density between that of cherry and maple. Edge treatments are typically stronger on more dense woods, but all three of these woods are sufficiently durable for furniture construction.

Late in 2007, the last of a series of courses was completed at Rosewood Studio. The last courses focused on detail work, inlay and small projects. One course, in particular, had a demi-lune table as the project. A prominent American woodworker, Garrett Hack, taught the course. Each student would need to complete a table while in the course.

A FASCINATION WITH CABINETS 163

The demi-lune table is unique in that the front apron rail is curved and wraps around the front and sides of the table to create a crescent-shaped tabletop. We had to create the angled tenons that attach the curved rail to the back legs by hand. This was an interesting exercise involving many calculations. A second course with Garrett Hack involved the design and build of a wall-mounted cabinet. The cabinet would be constructed of clear pine with a lapped cedar back and a raised cherry door panel. There was to be a single door on this cabinet. All the components of the small cabinet were created and shaped with hand tools. Each student had some artistic license to add additional elements to the design. This course provided me the training to be able to create wall cabinets.

Decorative wall cabinet I made during Garrett Hack course (2007)

During this period, blogging was also discovered. Blogging had become quite popular and consideration was given to writing posts about furniture created in my workshop. Posts could also be written about my methods of work, my woodworking philosophy as well as my furniture designs. This was very appealing to me since I enjoyed writing. A blog was created in early autumn 2007 and entries were posted, typically every three days or so. Each post would also include an image or two. The blog, **The Refined Edge**, began to grow in popularity and a considerable following was being developed. I continue to blog about woodworking today.

With a new emphasis on cabinets, new marketing channels would need to be developed. Since shipping cabinets of this size can get complicated and costly, it was preferable to establish a local market for the cabinets. My city is fairly large although not as large as nearby urban centers. The larger urban centers of Toronto and Montreal were a few hours away and transporting furniture on my own was a viable option. The challenge would be to educate people on the benefits of one of a kind, heirloom furniture and the customization that could be provided.

All these thoughts and ideas were racing through my mind. With my jewelry boxes, a few could easily be created on spec and eventually sold. The more popular models of jewelry boxes would be created. With my cabinets, this approach no longer made sense. Since there would be unique design and customization with each cabinet, they could not merely be produced on **(spec)** speculation. A commission would need to be acquired from a client along with a down payment for materials. This is the standard method of doing commission work. As well, there would be a formal contract signed both by the client and myself. The contract included completion dates as well as an accurate estimate of the cost of the cabinet. I also decided to offer both standalone cabinets and wall-mounted cabinets as products.

This would also be my seventh year of employment at HP. The job had helped me to recover financially from the dilemma faced a few years earlier.

By 2007, the additional cost of building our home was finally eliminated and we had reduced our mortgage payment to a more reasonable monthly payment. I continued to equip my workshop with more wall-mounted cabinets as well as a dedicated plane rack. The wall mounted plane rack design was modeled after existing designs. The hand planes would sit in compartments and would be angled so I could quickly grab the hand plane necessary for a task.

Dedicated hand plane rack for quick access of hand planes (2007)

Over the course of the year, a new piece of machinery was also acquired. I was informed of an opportunity to purchase a vintage wide bed jointer.

The vintage jointer, a **Wadkin Bursgreen**, had a 9.25 inch wide bed which was five feet long. It had been used in different workshops including Rosewood Studio. Most recently, it was no longer used and arrangements were made to purchase it. The jointer was solidly built and approximately fifty years old at the time. Thick sheet metal and solid cast components gave it heft. It had been upgraded to modern electrics with a new single-phase 3HP motor and modern starter switch. It would need to be disassembled to be brought back to my workshop.

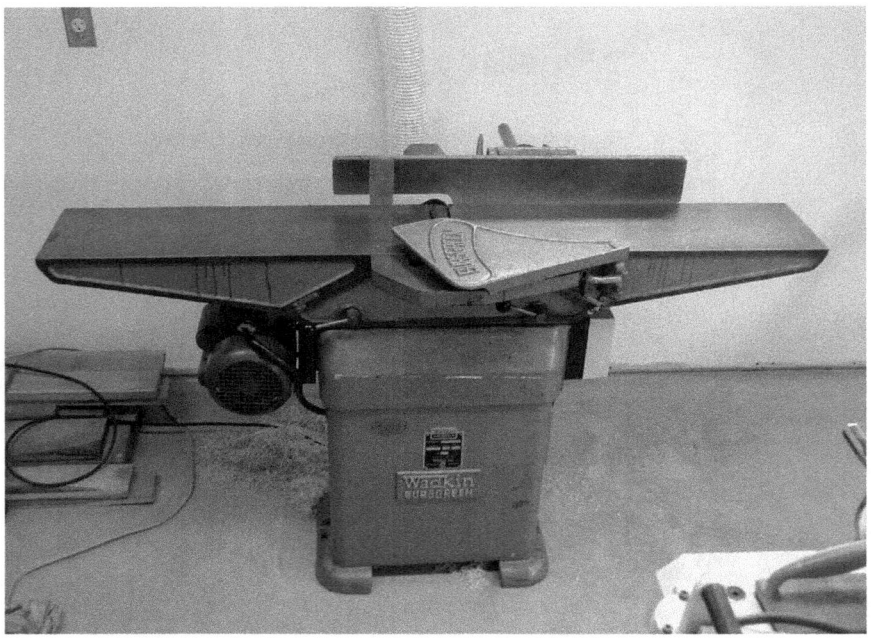

Antique jointer which was rebuilt and acquired in late 2007

The process of disassembling and re-assembling gave me the opportunity to adjust it, clean it, and lubricate internal components. I was ecstatic about the purchase since my only other jointer was a six-inch wide model. This new jointer would allow me to prepare the surfaces of much wider boards. In the past, wide boards would need to be ripped into narrower boards to fit the smaller jointer.

In mid-2008, another of the standalone cabinets was being designed and built. This particular one would have a much cleaner design and feature fully veneered front doors. I wanted to feature unique grain graphics on the doors. Assembling doors using frame and panel considerably reduced the size of the graphics of the panel. Fully veneered doors would allow more door area to display exciting figure. A fully veneered method of door construction would also provide me an exciting challenge. The sides and back were of conventional solid wood construction. The back was assembled using frame and panel construction to stay true to the James Krenov cabinet philosophy. He believed that the back of a piece of furniture should be just as well made and beautiful as the front.

Typically in modern furniture, the back of furniture is inexpensively put together since it is always assumed the furniture will be against a wall. A frame and panel back would instead be seen when the front doors are opened, adding to the interior beauty of a cabinet. Although this step involved considerably more work, the results were well worth it.

I designed and built the upper cabinet and then assembled the stand for a cabinet. Creating the cabinet and stand as separate units allowed me to make the stand more accurate in dimensions. The cabinet would perfectly conform to the base of the cabinet. The upper cabinet and stand were also designed to be separated for ease of transport and handling. This second cabinet would feature fewer drawers in the interior than the earlier cabinet. Instead, I wanted to create more space in which to display valuable art objects such as vases and bowls. The added interior height would allow three lower drawers, arranged in an asymmetric layout. Another feature of this cabinet would be the plain uniformity of the wood surfaces. A very light color was decided on and European Beech was used to accomplish this. European Beech does not have a pronounced grain pattern, instead it appears very plain. This was the desired effect for the cabinet. The only dramatic part of the cabinet was to be the exciting, matching graphics integral to the front doors. Lark Books featured the **Twin Plumes** cabinet in the forward of the **500 Cabinets** book.

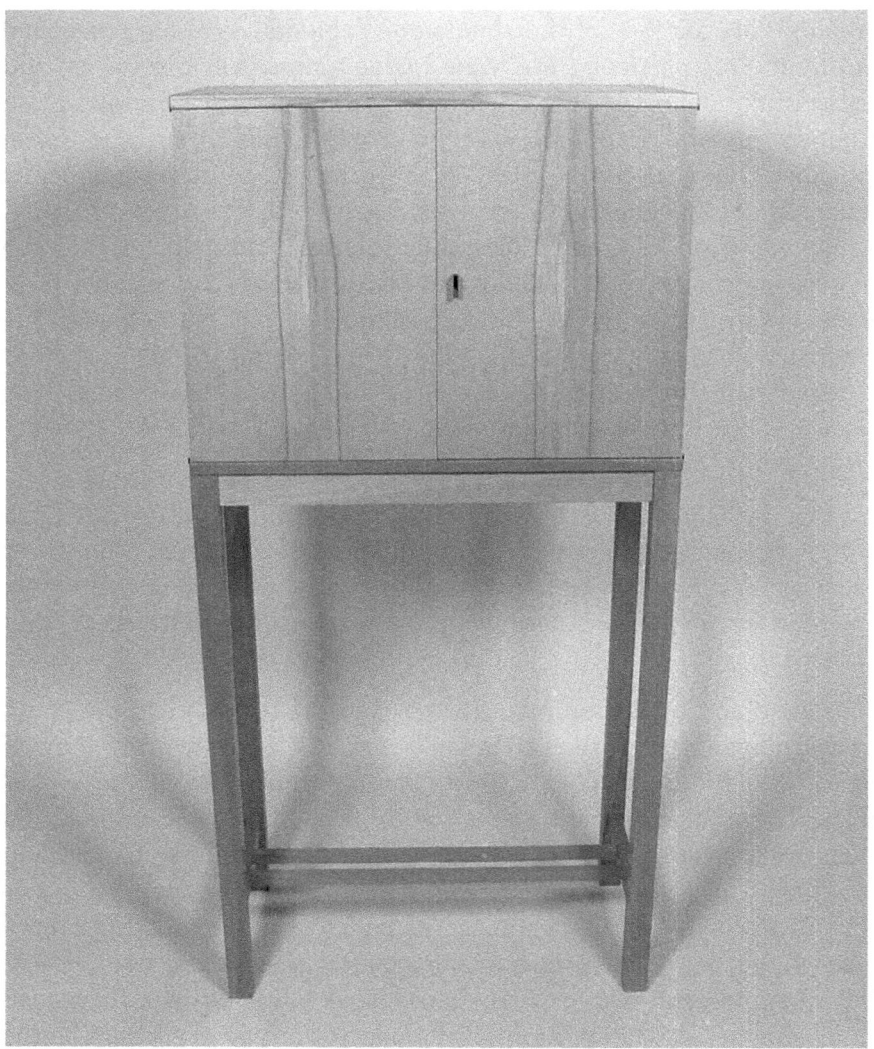

Twin Plumes, a European Beech cabinet with fully veneered door panels featuring unusual door graphics (2008)

Some unique bench jigs were also developed early in 2008. These jigs would plug into the round dog holes of a bench. They could be either mounted directly to a bench or attached to a planing board.

The bench jigs were a follow-on to the original system of bench jigs developed a few years earlier. I also designed and made new bench hooks and new shooting boards with attachments.

A system of bench jigs developed in my workshop (2008)

As a subscriber to **Fine Woodworking Magazine (FWW)**, I had an opportunity to write a submission for a magazine article. It was thought was that perhaps an article on my collection of bench jigs would be a good idea. A few days later a proposal for an article was written and submitted and then the wait began to hear back from FWW magazine. Their editorial staff reviews all submissions for magazine articles and picks the ones that are best suited.

A few weeks later, I was informed of the acceptance of my article. A date was scheduled for an editor from FWW to come to my workshop and photograph the jigs. It was also mentioned that the process of building the jigs would be photographed and it was expected that these jigs be built while FWW was at my workshop.

The photography was done and a few months later a new FWW article called **4 Bench Jigs for Handplanes** was published in two versions of the magazine. I have since had other articles about my work published in other magazines.

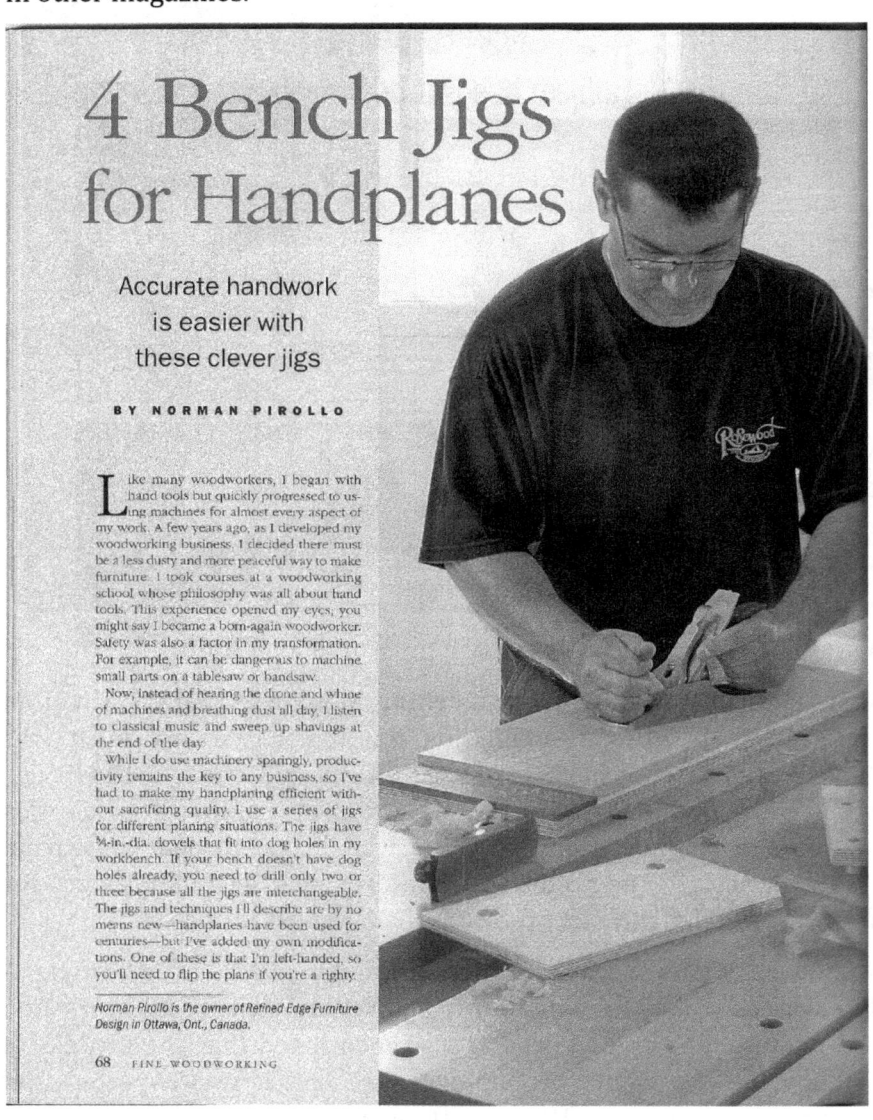

The author featured in a Fine Woodworking Magazine article on various bench jigs. Courtesy Fine Woodworking Issue No. 202

Using bench jig and hand planes to create small parts (2008)

I continued to seek other methods of marketing my work. Over the years and through various magazine articles, fairly good exposure has been gained. Exposure is critical to being successful as a furniture maker. Advertising of my business also began locally where business cards were handed out at every opportunity. A local woodworking group held a furniture exhibition and competition in the fall **Wood Objects 2008** where entrants would be able to exhibit a piece of furniture. A jury panel selected the entries. The competition awarded multiple winners in different categories. This was an excellent form of exposure for me. I entered the first year with a standalone cabinet and entered a table in the second year. Similar competitions were also held in other regions where my entry could be shipped to and shown for the duration of the exhibition. Opportunities were also sought where high-end crafts and furniture would be exhibited, all in the name of exposure.

Another success story was to be published in three different books on furniture designs and woodworking including **500 Cabinets, Studio Furniture: Today's Leading Woodworkers** and **Rooted: Creating a Sense of Place: Contemporary Studio Furniture**.

"Standing Tall" standalone cabinet entry at Wood Objects 2008

My entry was submitted as part of a call for entry and was fortunately accepted in each of these books. The exposure gained from this type of press can be invaluable to a furniture maker. The opportunity was also provided to exhibit some of my furniture at an annual exhibition of furniture of **Rosewood Studio** current students and alumni.

The positive side effects of working exclusively with hand tools are the efficient methods of work a person develops over time. Along with this, new jigs and tools are developed to work more efficiently. With this in mind, I developed a bench tool that improved my work. The problem addressed was how to hold work while hand planing it. Specifically, how to hold a piece of wood flat against a workbench surface when there is no tail vise in the bench. I tackled this dilemma and developed an adjustable surface vise with an extremely low profile. The vise also needed to have a durable coarse and fine adjustment mechanism. Through trial and error and some ingenuity, a few issues were worked out. The surface vise design was refined and the production version is manufactured exclusively in metal. The surface vise is currently manufactured and marketed through a large Canadian tool manufacturer **Veritas Tools**. We share the patent for its design.

One of the prototypes of the surface mount tail vise (2008)

THREE STRIKES

"Change is the law of life. And those who look only to the past or present are certain to miss the future"

John F. Kennedy

LATE IN THE YEAR 2008 I was away on a short vacation with my spouse. Upon my return, a phone call was received from my current manager. He informed me of bad news; my position was being eliminated in a few weeks. It was somewhat surprising to hear this news. Although aware of a few support staff being downsized over the past year and a colleague of mine losing his employment at HP, I never thought this would affect my job.

This was my eighth year of employment at Hewlett-Packard and I was enjoying the job. I also felt fortunate to have the opportunity to work a condensed, short work week and to be able to work from home. The short work week allowed me to work at my business. It would be almost impossible to find other, similar employment. I also enjoyed the camaraderie of working with my support team based in Atlanta, Georgia. After the initial shock, it was mentioned that paperwork of my severance package would be received by mail. In the meantime, my job remained for a few more weeks. I would continue to perform my job and then begin a severance period. In this time, other employment at HP could be sought. This relieved some of the sting at being downsized, only to find out that there were not many positions available.

If there were positions available, I would need to relocate close to a larger facility. This gave me time to think about my future. This would also be the third downsizing experienced over a twelve year period. After discussing with my spouse, we agreed that maybe I should give serious thought about continuing in the computer industry. This would be my thirtieth year in the industry and the time might be right to finally walk away.

It was somewhat difficult to continue at my job and it was done with sadness. There was awkwardness in my team since other team members were aware of my predicament. Usually, in downsizing, an employee is asked to leave immediately, but this was not my case. I continued to contribute to the team for the next few weeks. Once the severance package papers were received, they were signed and returned and my period of severance begun.

This news also threw a wrench into my woodworking business since this would cause me to be completely dependent on my self-employment earnings. I welcomed the challenge, however, and repeated the old adage **when one door closes, another door opens**. The situation was accepted in stride and it would be seen what happened next as it was no longer definite I would continue in the computer industry.

The other dilemma now faced was that of seeking other employment. Most, if not all computer related jobs are five day a week jobs with additional commuting time involved. The end result would be that only weekends were available to work at my woodworking business. This would be almost impossible to manage since I would need to spend time with my spouse and do everything else that people do on weekends. It was simply not appealing to me.

My only option now would be to work hard at my woodworking business during the severance period. I would at the very least, determine if my business would provide me with sufficient income to survive on. The typical severance package for my years of service was salary and benefits for a six-month period. This equates to being paid for six months. I was determined to work hard at my woodworking business for as long as one year.

Hopefully, it could be grown substantially in this period. My cost of living would also need to be reduced over this period to ensure I could live comfortably for a year. My purchases would consist only of materials that were absolutely necessary to operate my business. Tool and machinery expenses were placed on hold until further notice. The next few months were tumultuous with a considerable amount of hand wringing. There was not one day where I did not think about my future. With the safety of regular employment gone, self-employment slowly became more of a reality.

The year 2009 brought forth many new ideas. The regular income from jewelry box sales and my Woodworking Course CD became necessary to survive financially. A singular focus on display cabinets was no longer an option, although there was much more time available to devote to my business. The extra time would allow me to continue to develop new furniture designs as well as maintain the jewelry box business. The demand for cigar humidors had completely dropped off at this time and making these would no longer be a concern.

Instead of a single focus on display cabinets, an emphasis on contemporary furniture designs also began to make more sense. I wanted to design contemporary tables as well. It was important for me to distinguish myself as a furniture designer. Designs would need to be considerably more interesting than what was available in the furniture market. Designing a series of tables would be a radical departure for me since I had developed a reputation as a maker of Krenov-styled cabinets.

Once my final weeks of employment at HP ended, the severance period began. Within this period, the option to seek employment within HP was available. A few inquiries were made over a period of a few weeks, but the few positions available involved five day a week employment. This would completely disrupt my goal of self-employment or even running a part-time business. I had made too much progress in working towards self-employment and developing a woodworking business to abandon this now. Juggling a full-time five day a week job and my business would not work for me. It was also difficult to continually switch gears from a five day work week to a two-day business.

Since there is a large component of design in my furniture making, the weekly transition from work to furniture making would also be non-productive. A decision would need to be made!

I never did make the decision in that first year of leaving HP. Simply continuing to make furniture kept me continually busy and new employment was never sought. Periodically, I was contacted about job opportunities and contract work but never acted on the requests. Computer contract work was another option to me. I could work full-time at a contract for a few months and then return to my business. Although this sounded appealing, in discussions with other contract workers it was discovered that very often contracts are extended. It is expected that the contractor continue with the contract. Reputation is very critical in the world of contract work.

If a contractor is deemed to be unreliable with regard to contract extensions, future opportunities available to them vanish. On the subject of reputation, it was also discovered that the world of contract recruiters was close-knit. Abandoning my woodworking business for months at a time would also cause negative issues in business continuity. In light of this, contract work became less of an option.

A few table designs began to occupy me in the early part of 2009. Combining wood and metal was of interest to me. The appeal of console and hall tables also appealed to me. The narrow profile of this type of table involved a smaller table top where a seamless top could be created. In a conventional table, a wide top would involve gluing up narrower boards. In my market research, I discovered that console and hall tables addressed a niche which was not very well served. The console tables on the market were mostly imported and similar in style. I could distinguish myself as a domestic maker and create new, exciting console table designs. Console tables and hall tables are essentially similar in design aside from their dimensions. This feature appealed to me since this versatility would enable me to address two markets. Within a few weeks, a hall table was designed which incorporated both metal and wood. The metal components would be stand offs which elevated and separated the top from the underlying legs and rail structure.

The top would appear to be floating. Metal was also used for the rails of the hall table. This created a balance of wood and metal and added to the appeal of the table. There would be no curves in the table; instead straight or tapered components were desired. This feature added to the contemporary style.

Newly designed mahogany hall table with wood and metal (2009)

The radical departure from display cabinets to hall tables and the excellent feedback of the new design encouraged me to pursue other table designs. The design of demi-lune tables always appealed to me. Although a conventional demi-lune design appears straightforward, the complexity of creating a curved apron and attaching legs to it was complex. Being fond of the combination of metal with wood in my previous table; I worked on a demi-lune design that would incorporate both these mediums. The first demi-lune table design featured a highly figured birds' eye maple top with tapered legs. The tapered legs were attached to the table top with metal components. The need for an apron rail was also eliminated in this design.

The tapered legs were a combination of cherry with holly feet. It was found that the woods contrasted well with the metal. The design was also unique, innovative and very contemporary.

Contemporary demi-lune design with wood and metal (2009)

A second demi-lune table design utilized a different approach. It would have tubular metal legs that attached to both the table top and a lower section. The table top was figured wood. Two versions were made, one with a darker lacewood top and the other with a lighter flame birch top. This design was not quite as elegant as the previous demi-lune table, but it was very contemporary. I prided myself on new and unique contemporary designs. These designs would hopefully bring attention to my furniture making business. Another table design had an ovoid table top instead of the demi-lune design. The table was designed as a side table. A uniquely shaped top and slender, tapered legs were attached using metal components.

The metal components were designed to be a feature of the table. This particular table along with one of the demi-lune tables was destined for a furniture gallery in Toronto. For a period of months in early 2009, my focus was on these table designs. An art exhibition was entered which took place in June of 2009. This was a prestigious art show that was also open to other forms of fine craft. It was to be held at a large downtown convention center in Toronto, Ontario. I feverishly worked at creating a variety of furniture pieces to showcase my business at this exhibition.

The design of the earlier table designs was partially motivated by this exhibition. I had a booth and over a few days was able to talk about my work with many of the thousands of visitors to the show. This was to be my first experience with my own booth at such a show. Although the expenses incurred with travel, lodging, booth registration and lighting were high; I viewed this as an excellent experience for future shows. The feedback received motivated me to continue to go forward with my furniture business, **Refined Edge Design**.

An interesting twist of fortune also occurred in 2009. As part of the design process for the tables, scale models of each table were created. The scale models would be sufficiently large to be well photographed. The detail would also be prominently featured. The scale models would be exact scale models of larger full-scale furniture designs.

As a member of a provincial craft organization, I was informed of upcoming events and calls for entry. A touring exhibition of furniture and craft was to be held over the course of a few months in mid-2009. A scale model of the ovoid table was submitted. The scaled down table, although very small, could provide functionality as a stand for a small art object. It was exhilarating to find out my entry was accepted and it would be part of this touring exhibition. The small scale ovoid table would be exhibited at multiple craft venues in Eastern Ontario over a few months. I was also invited to speak about my furniture work at one of the events. This positive experience opened my eyes to a new opportunity. Scale pieces of furniture could be created to serve two functions. They could either be scale models for larger furniture or serve as unique, small art objects.

The scaled down furniture would also enable me to experiment with furniture designs without investing considerable time and materials. If the small-scaled furniture had an appealing aesthetic, I could go ahead and create the full-scale version. Working at this approach for a while, a series of scaled down furniture models were created. This motivated me since my productivity rapidly increased. In a short time, designs could be fleshed out and their appeal determined. Using this approach, the scaled down furniture models were entered in local exhibitions. The pieces were entered in the category of sculptural work.

Towards the final months of 2009, a submission was once again made to the prestigious **Wood Objects 2009** local furniture exhibition and competition. My entry the previous year was a standalone cabinet. This year a contemporary styled console table was designed. I wanted to enter a table that would be a challenge to create and would push the boundaries of my skills. This console table would also incorporate curved surfaces instead of the linear surfaces of my previous hall table design. The curves would provide a contemporary, organic aesthetic.

The design process was begun with sketches and drawings and progressed to creating maquettes. Maquettes are very small scale models of furniture. The scale is so they can be rapidly put together using scraps of wood. The maquette I created from my final drawing was not as appealing as originally envisioned. The narrow base of the table did not seem right; issues of stability came into play. Since this was a very small-scale model, it was simply inverted and then it made more sense. Stability was no longer an issue as the base was now wider at the bottom. This demonstrates the power of using maquettes in the design process. Maquettes provide a 3-D view of the design as well as pointing out construction deficiencies, stability issues or technical challenges.

Scale model or maquette used in the design of curved hall table (2009). This is the original design before inverting the base.

The console table build went well. Many challenges and obstacles were faced with the design. Both metal and wood were combined in this design, along with some complex technical details. The table was completed with two weeks to spare before the exhibition. It drew considerable attention since it was an unusual, organic design.

Console table with inverted base, curved surfaces, and metal components entered in Wood Objects 2009.

Early in 2010, an acquaintance was made with a local artist. He was on the jury of an exhibition entered a few months earlier. At the time, I considered him a mentor since he encouraged me to enter art competitions with my small sculptural pieces. At one point, a departure from functionality was made and I instead created non-objective sculptural pieces using wood as the primary medium. Metal, glass, and wood were combined in the next series of sculptures. **Terry Sametz** also suggested to me the advantages of joining a local arts group that he was on the board of. I joined and this launched my entry into the art world. Over the next months, a few art exhibitions were entered with my new series of conceptual wood sculptures. As a consequence, my visibility and reputation as a wood sculptor within the local arts community was growing.

Wood sculpture which began my entry into the local art world (2010)

I soon began to enjoy creating these sculptures. Since sculptural work lacked any functionality, I was free to focus on form instead. Contrasting and complementary woods were often combined in unique designs. The art group had also set up a glass display case for me to exhibit my sculptures.

Later in 2010, the possibility of featuring exciting wood graphics as a form of art was explored. The art would be hung from a wall as wood art. Resawn veneers could be used as the focal point for the art. Highly figured veneers assembled together would form an abstract composition. The veneer components would be assembled in a wood frame to provide depth. Within a few days, a preliminary form of art was created using this technique. It was entered in an upcoming art exhibition where it received positive feedback. This encouraged me to create more of these wall art pieces. This was to be my entry to the art world. I was also invited to exhibit my new wood art pieces at a local venue, **Santé Gallery**. This venue would rotate art on a monthly basis. The exhibition was given a title and my art would share wall space with another artist's work.

A few weeks were invested in the creation of a new body of work for the Santé Gallery exhibition, held for five consecutive weeks in December 2010. In this time, I had also begun to win awards in both local and regional juried art exhibitions. During the 2010-11 period, both my wood sculptures and my new wall art pieces were entered in several exhibitions. This series of wall art featured the natural color of the wood veneers selected. Although the natural wood colors were intriguing, my opinion was that by infusing color into the wood the wall art would have more dramatic appeal. I could experiment with a wide variety of colors. During the year 2011, a new body of work was created using dye infused colors and this wall art was then entered in local juried exhibitions. The response was enthusiastic and people were genuinely drawn to the wall art.

The color brought out the depth and enhanced the figure of the wood. The woods used were highly figured and in most cases a unique graphic pattern could be distinguished. This new work appealed to lovers of wood and art. They could now have wood art hanging in their homes. This work also validated me as a serious wood artist in the local arts community. The concept of wood art hanging from a wall was unique and novel in the art world.

Wall art using highly figured veneers, infused with color (2011)

WoodSkills

"If a window of opportunity appears, don't pull down the shade"
Tom Peters

EARLY IN THE YEAR 2011 I was made aware of a government sponsored business-training program. After some deliberation, the decision was made to meet with a recruiting agent. We discussed my background, my goals, and what I was doing at the moment. The program was an intensive business course. Although I had some business education prior to this, it was not at the level of this training. All facets of starting and operating a business would be taught. Guest instructors from the business community were brought in to teach; individuals that had extensive expertise with business start-ups.

The interview went well and I was asked to draft a proposal for a new business idea. Three weeks were provided to accomplish this and then to submit it for review. Shortly afterwards, a panel would inform me of my acceptance. They were seeking people that had been out of the workforce for at least two years. Although I met all the criteria, it was necessary to arrive at a new business idea over the three week period. Within this three week period, business ideas were tossed around. With my skill set in mind and knowing what I enjoyed doing, it was narrowed down to a specific woodworking business. The criteria stated that this had to be a new business.

Building on the Woodworking Course CD created a few years earlier, I contemplated creating a business dedicated to teaching online woodworking. At the time, I was convinced this was an idea worth pursuing to address the growing niche of online learning. The idea was to assemble many online tutorials as well as woodworking courses. The online tutorials would each address a specific aspect of woodworking. Woodworking plans would also be offered as part of the business. With the experience of developing my original Woodworking Course CD, creating the tutorials would not present much of a challenge. I could handle the technical aspect of delivery. The challenge would be to create a new business around this idea and the business program would help me in this regard. Within a short period of time, a proposal would need to be drafted and submitted. I would then be informed of my acceptance in the program. The next three weeks were hectic. A general outline of the proposal they were seeking was provided to me. Specific questions would need to be answered and serious thought given to this new business idea. A portion of the proposal was dedicated to market research. It was also asked of me to determine the market potential of the business idea.

After answering the questions with my best responses, the proposal was completed. An advantage of drafting a proposal is that it forces you to think hard about your business idea. The process is much like drafting a business plan. The proposal was submitted well within the deadline. I waited to hear back from the business specialists in the group. They would determine if the idea was viable or not. There was intense competition to enroll in this program and only the best, most promising business ideas were accepted. A few days later, I was informed of my acceptance into the program. My next step would be to meet with the business specialist assigned to me. At the meeting, we discussed the proposal and pointed questions were asked. It was mentioned to me that furniture related businesses are typically not accepted since they did not have good success with this type of business in the past. It was pointed to the business specialist that the new business was not to make furniture but to provide online learning about the furniture making process. Delivery would be both online and in DVD format.

It was mentioned that I currently made furniture but was dependent on client commissions. A more regular source of income was necessary. My background in computer software development also helped considerably in having my proposal accepted. The training began a week later and it was to be a nine-month intensive program. Attendance in class for a few hours each day was necessary. Since the training would impact my woodworking business, I could still back out if necessary. Instead, the challenge was welcomed and I began to attend classes. This would be a rare opportunity for me to receive a free business education. While in the program, a small amount of money was paid to the students as an incentive to join the program.

The first few classes were introductory in nature, where a few instructors would rotate through each class. Each of these instructors had a business specialty. Topics such as business plan development, accounting, bookkeeping, social media, business structure and market research were discussed. The course was an eye opener for me; prior to this I did not have much formal business training. My motivation to attend each class was high as each topic would affect my business somehow. The topics discussed would also help me in my furniture making business since they were generic in nature. After a few classes that discussed writing a business plan, we were instructed to begin developing our own business plan. The individual classes covered different components of business plans which we would implement in our own business plan.

I soon began to write the business plan. Until this time, very little thought was placed on business plans; I was of the opinion they were only useful to acquire business financing from a financial institution. This was not the case since business plans map out the direction of a business. Market research is a large part of a business plan as is the structure of a business. With each lecture, an appreciation of the power and usefulness of a business plan was increasing. My project was to write a business plan and this began a few weeks into the business-training program. We had a deadline to develop the business plan and it would then be reviewed. The review would determine if we should continue with the program or not.

There was a large emphasis placed on the business plan. The risk of being terminated from the program was a great motivation to work hard at the business plan.

Throughout this period, thought was given of a name for my new business. From past experience, it was best to have a short name, one that was easy to remember and spell. Another consideration was a domain name for the business. In the past, this was not necessary, but today a web site presence is a large part of a business' success. Since my business was predominantly an online business, the name of the business would need to meet the following criteria. A concise easily remembered name, a name relevant to the type of business, and the availability of the domain name were the criteria that I followed.

Finding a name for the business proved to be one of the largest challenges over the next few months. It was not necessary to come up with a final business name until the last months of the program. To motivate me to go forward, I was keen on establishing a business name. For expediency, the business name requirement was put aside while continuing to give it thought.

The business class lectures were extremely informational and the added value that the instructors brought was invaluable. They had each started or help start multiple businesses and had much expertise to share with the class. Many of the students in the program had innovative ideas whereas a few were starting generic businesses. My business was one of the most innovative businesses since the major component would be the online delivery of educational material. The premise for the whole business was Internet-based learning.

The business training lectures were held over a six-month period. The final three months of the nine-month program would be to begin implementing the business plan. While attending the business program lectures, a decision was made to hold off on any woodworking. Later in 2011, woodworking resumed after the series of lectures had been completed. In the last part of 2011, work also began on two commissions and some wall art.

Large wall art commission using figured woods completed in 2011

I finally decided on a name for the business. After much soul-searching and research on domain name availability, the business name decided on was **WoodSkills**. Interestingly enough, the domain was available. It is most difficult to find an unregistered domain name today; it seems that every conceivable name has been registered. The name was registered, both as a domain name and business name. The name was to the point, concise, easily spelled and relevant.

During the next phase of the program, a new web site was developed. I wanted this web site to follow up to date web site development standards. Since developing my last web site, the process had changed considerably. A new, structured programming language had been developed specifically for web sites. The decision was made to develop the web site myself since it would be expensive to have such a complex, customized web site professionally created. My business would involve much ongoing customization of the web site; this would be continual since new tutorials would be added and updated, and courseware and free content added. It became obvious that I would need to successfully create and manage my own web site as part of the business.

The first step would be to learn new web site development software involving Cascading Style Sheets or **CSS**. A book was purchased on the subject as well as purchasing new software to accomplish this. Over the next few weeks, I hunkered down and taught myself to create a modern, dynamic web site. Web site design and development began shortly afterward.

The web site would need to be designed to be easily updated. Products such as tutorials, articles and courses would continually be added. Other criteria of the web site would be easy access, a common header and footer on each page, E-commerce capability, adaptability to different screen widths and mobile readiness. The new web site was completed a few weeks later and I began to populate it with tutorials and courses. The original Woodworking Course was also upgraded to be in video format, a lengthy process occurring over a period of months. Work on individual tutorials also began. The tutorials would focus on hand tool techniques. Woodworking project plans were also included.

After having successfully implemented the new **WoodSkills** web site, I proceeded to learn new skills such as CAD. CAD or **Computer Aided Design** knowledge would help me considerably in providing plans for projects. Highly detailed and rendered CAD drawings along with parts lists would be drawn up for the jigs and machines built in my workshop. An example of a complex plan involving considerable CAD drawings is a router table I designed and made. The router table was designed and built over a period of days. A design was sought which could be put together in days instead of weeks. Commonly available lumber was used except for the fence and table top components. The construction featured torsion box technology. All the plans offered through "WoodSkills" are machines or jigs I have built and continue to use in my own workshop.

It was also critical to learn how to produce videos to implement in the new version of my woodworking course and upcoming tutorials. My focus for late 2011 and all of 2012 was entirely on developing WoodSkills as a viable business. The business program ended in December of 2011 and in the last few months we were expected to reach defined milestones. Monthly sales were expected to grow month over month. We had to hit the ground running with our business. The business adviser assigned to each of us would visit us to ensure we were following the business plan, and not heading off in a different direction. It was expected that I maintain bookkeeping records, begin marketing, advertise and make sales.

New WoodSkills Instructional Courseware logo, shown at right (2011)

My sales through WoodSkills were trickling in and an emphasis was placed on marketing soon after populating the web site with a few tutorials, plans, and course. A selection of free articles was also included to provide content at the web site. Search engines rank web sites on content among other criteria; although this is another topic for another day. The business program soon wound down and I graduated. Contact was also maintained with my business adviser over the next year or so. The business education was invaluable to me and the timing could not be better since I had been seeking new opportunities to generate revenue.

WoodSkills Certificate issued to Woodworking Course students

Furniture Design + Build

"To succeed in your mission, you must have single-minded devotion to your goal"

A. P. J. Abdul Kalam

THE NEXT TWO YEARS would be hectic for me. I now had two businesses to manage and grow. Business resumed at my furniture making business, **Refined Edge Design**, and work began on two standalone cabinet commissions. Commission work that had been placed on hold could now be resumed. Until now, development of WoodSkills with a focus on the start-up phase had been a priority. Since WoodSkills and Refined Edge Design both involved woodworking, they dovetailed well together. I could cross-pollinate and channel efforts placed into each of the businesses into the other.

The tutorials and plans offered through WoodSkills were derived from techniques used in the creation of furniture in my own workshop. The furniture would be created through Refined Edge Design. Beginning in 2012, "White Mountain Design" was placed on hold and the focus shifted to "Refined Edge Design" and "WoodSkills" instead. The jewelry box business had slowed down considerably since the end of the recession, although the occasional order trickled in. An emphasis on furniture making was now my priority. I thoroughly enjoyed designing and creating furniture as it made use of all my previous and new skills.

Display Cabinet using highly figured Ambrosia Maple veneers (2012)

The console tables designed earlier also encouraged me to pursue the creation of this type of furniture. Occasional tables such as console and hall tables were not nearly as complex to create as standalone cabinets. As was determined two years earlier, there was a niche for upscale versions of console and hall tables. The condo market had also grown considerably over the past few years and there was a demand for compact furniture. Narrow profile tables could be placed in a living room, entrance or hallway and not interfere much with the space. During this time, working with CAD also increased. Instead of drawing by hand and then creating a mockup; furniture designs could instead be drawn on a computer and then rendered. The rendering process provided a 3-D view of the furniture. It could be rotated and it was easy to determine if the proportions and design were aesthetically pleasing. The CAD process quickened the design process and also allowed me to create furniture plans. The initial CAD plans offered through WoodSkills were for a display cabinet.

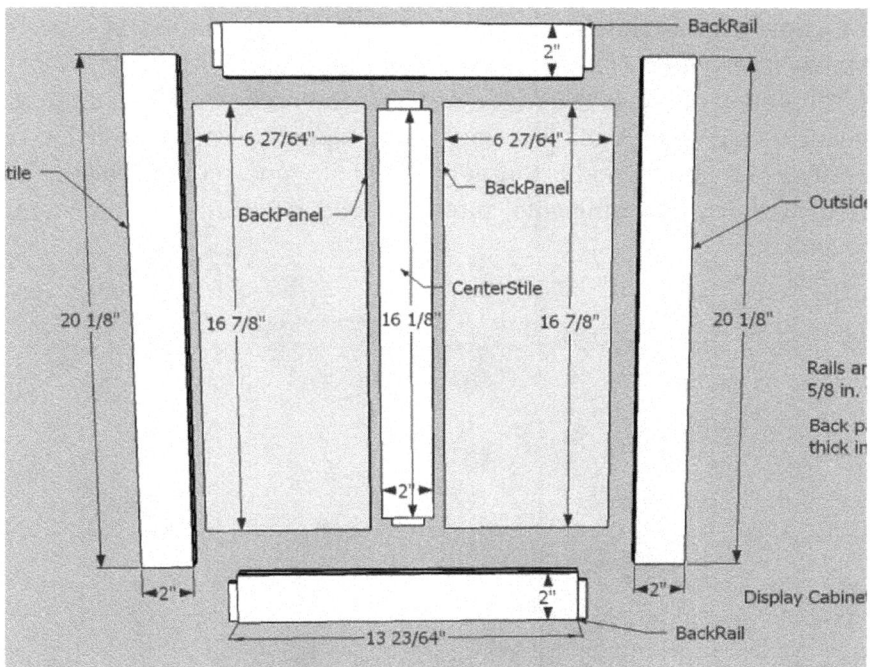

CAD drawings for display cabinet and back panel components (2012)

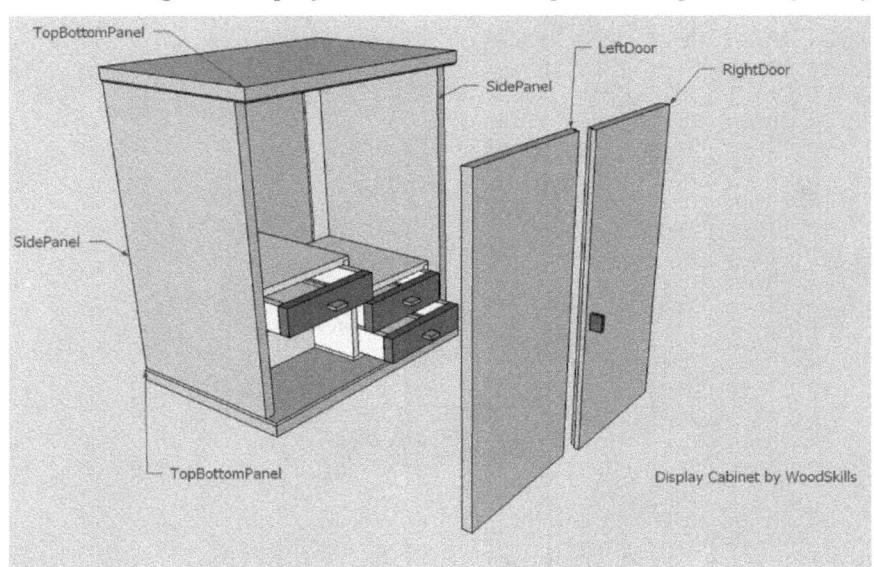

CAD drawings for display cabinet, an exploded view of cabinet (2012)

In this period, development of my wood art also continued. I began to create larger wood sculptures as well as wall art. With a new, more exciting body of work, it became possible to enter several exhibitions over the next two years. The increased exposure encouraged me to continue pursuing wood art. A new series of wood sculptures utilized the technique of infusing color into the wood, originally developed for my wall art.

Contemporary wood sculpture with dye infused color and highly figured wood (2012).

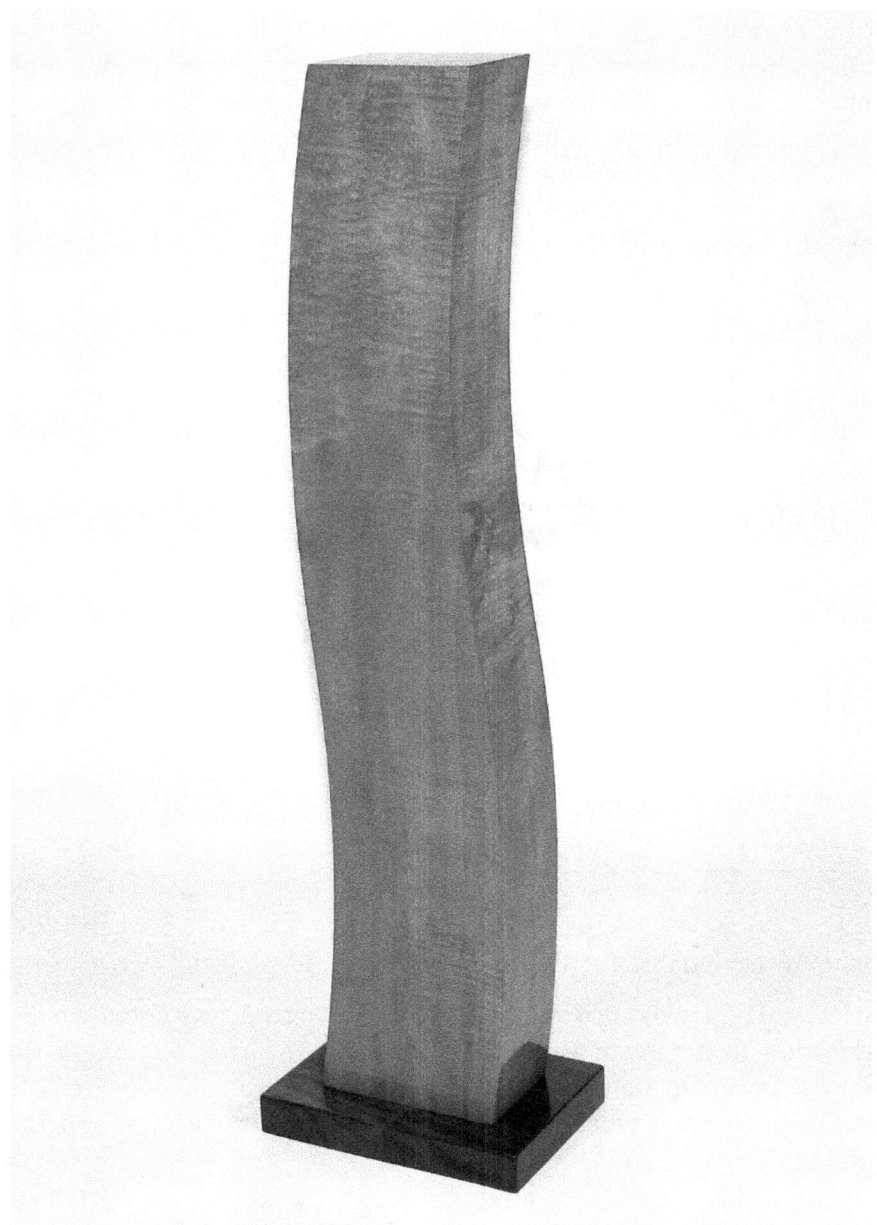

Wood sculpture using dye infused color in highly figured wood (2013).

With increased exposure and the creation of more interesting sculptures and wall art, several juried competitions were also entered. This step is typical for many artists and results were positive for me. Late in 2012, notification was received that I was a finalist for a very prestigious NICHE Award. A sculpture entered was one of five sculptures selected from across North America. I had also begun to win other art awards in this two-year period of 2012-13.

Niche Award Finalist Certificate for a sculpture I entered (2013)

In late 2012 I was also ecstatic about having been granted a solo exhibition in a City of Ottawa Art Gallery. The solo exhibition **Go Figure!** occurred in the spring of 2013 and brought considerable attention to my artwork from local art curators, collectors, and the public.

Exhibition card for Go Figure! exhibition (April, May 2013). Wood art featuring highly figured woods with infused dye color.

Author at the Go Figure! exhibition on opening night (April 2013)

Advertising for Refined Edge Design in interior design mags (2012)

Another benefit of my art exposure would be the increased attention to my furniture designs from the local community. My acceptance into a very prominent local gallery contributed greatly to local exposure. I also cross-pollinated techniques developed for my art to my furniture designs. Exposure of my furniture designs also became a priority. Opportunities were sought to show my furniture during this period. A smaller standalone cabinet created, **Standing Tall**, was ideal for this purpose. It was shown at different venues since it was small enough to easily transport. The detail of the cabinet and stand would sufficiently demonstrate my skills and generate dialogue about my work.

Development of a new series of console and hall tables had also begun during the 2012-13 period. The design of the tables would combine metal and wood. It was necessary to follow criteria necessary. Interchangeable table tops and legs, colored metal components and simplicity of design were criteria. The initial designs were hall tables, but subsequent designs were console tables. I wanted to introduce innovation in the designs, to do something that had not been previously done.

In recent years, I had been aware of a large Interior Design Show held annually in Toronto, Canada. **IDS** was and currently is the largest Interior Design Show held in Canada. As part of the show, there is a dedicated maker space, **Studio North**, set up in one large area of the exhibition hall. A juried selection process is used to determine which designers would participate each year. To promote emerging designers, the booth costs for Studio North were kept lower than in the main area of the show. Along with lower entry costs, the booths were turn key with hard white walls and carpeting provided. The organizers seek a gallery type setting with uniform booth designs. I had not applied in the previous year due to my commitment of establishing WoodSkills. The expense of participating in this show was also quite high. There would be booth fees, travel expenses, lodging, food and other booth setup costs such as lighting.

In light of my new focus on furniture designs, I entered the 2014 edition of the show **IDS14**, held in January of 2014. Notification of my acceptance to Studio North was received in late summer of 2013 with a few months to prepare for the exhibition.

At this time, I had already designed two models of hall and console tables in anticipation of being accepted. These models had solid wood tops in either a straight edge rectangular configuration or a curved edge configuration. The console and hall tables would also feature a unique design of two legs instead of four, along with a single rail at the bottom. The structure of the table was sufficiently stable with two legs and hardwood feet. There were now a few months to determine if these were the tables to bring or should a completely new series of console tables be designed. I began work on a similar design but with a different table top approach. Laminated tops were used instead of solid tops.

New contemporary hall table deign with two legs and solid top (2013)

The laminated tops allowed me to introduce a variety of colors to the console table design. The steel legs were powder coated to introduce color. The original legs were nickel-plated steel, but my preference was black legs. I had experimented with a variety of colors for the steel legs but decided on black. Instead, it was decided to introduce color into the laminated top of the table design. There would be a selection of trendy colors available. The substrate was assembled from two thick slabs of Baltic Birch plywood with a distinct under-bevel to mask the thickness of the top. The legs were powder-coated black for the two tables **Nuovo Console Tables** introduced at the show.

Nuovo Console Table with laminated top and black powder-coated legs, introduced at IDS14. ©2014 Marc Lavoie - Courtesy Marc Lavoie Photography.

Being part of the Studio North area of IDS14 was a marketing coup for me. The exposure generated from this single design show was larger than a year's worth of advertising. **Studio North** had developed a reputation as the place to see new and exciting furniture designs.

I could not be more excited in the weeks and months leading up to the show. There were several marketing steps necessary before the show since there would be considerable media attention at the show. Media people are always seeking new and interesting designs to write about. A press kit was necessary, new business cards prepared, along with work on the logistics of getting the furniture to the show in a different city. Custom DVD disks were prepared with detailed specifications of the console tables along with higher resolution images. These would be made available to design houses, furniture retailers and the media.

A new floor lamp design was also introduced at IDS14. The floor lamp, **Versicolor**, combined wood and metal in different configurations. Components of the lamp could be interchanged to select a both a wood type and a powder coated metal color. Many weeks were invested in the lamp design as well as research into lamp electrics and certification. The wiring was completely concealed through the metal and wood post. The lampshades were also interchangeable. The lamp design was very contemporary and fitted with LED Eco lamps. This was my first lamp design and the feedback from visitors to my booth was enthusiastic. Since the size of the Studio North booth was limited to 5 feet X 5 feet, the floor lamp could be placed in the corner of the booth.

Versicolor Floor Lamp combining wood, metal introduced at IDS14

The show was a success and the media attention received was rewarding. Judging from the feedback of visitors to the show, my table design and floor lamp were a hit. Upon my return, I was pleased to find that the local media had picked up on my furniture design and featured my tables in a story on local designers at IDS14. This feature story generated considerable interest in my furniture designs.

With the success of IDS14 behind me, the decision was made to apply for next year's version **IDS15**. Notification of my acceptance was received in the early summer of 2014 and work began on a new furniture design. Since participating in IDS14 with a table design, it was decided to do something completely different for the next show. The organizers of the IDS show like returning designers to bring new designs. This was completely understood as Studio North prides itself on new, leading-edge designs.

Over the years, I had always wanted to design a chair. Until this time, I had not designed a chair, assuming the complexity of it all was too challenging. Chair design is somewhat different from other furniture designs. Most furniture is fairly static and is simply situated in a room with little to no interaction. Chairs, on the other hand, are dynamic in that people sit and introduce stresses to the joinery and components. Ergonomics and chair standards are also factors in the design.

I gave this some thought and decided to accept my own challenge of designing and building a chair for IDS15. As part of my application, the type of furniture to be shown at IDS15 had to be specified. The type of chair decided on was a lounge chair. It was to be a very contemporary design and radically different from other, existing chairs in the market. The design process began.

Over the next weeks several different designs were tossed around, sketched and drawn on paper. I was fortunate to have a small captive group of friends and family to bounce the designs off of. The design process progressed from paper to CAD drawings, complete with colored furniture components. A few designs were rendered and a poll was set up among family and friends to determine which design was most appealing. This provided me with an idea for a preliminary mockup.

The first few designs were not exciting enough. It would need to be a more radical chair design to motivate and excite me to design and build it. I continued with the design process using CAD. The design process is an iterative one where each design utilizes elements of the previous design. The lounge chair design envisioned was to be a departure from conventionally designed lounge chairs. It would ideally have fewer components that the standard chair but be equally as strong. Since IDS demands the latest and most exciting designs, I gave myself carte blanche to do something radical. The next version of the chair was completely different from that which was earlier rendered and shown to friends and family.

With a little engineering, I worked on a new design with a wood structure that would be held together with a single bolt. A rough sketch was drafted and work began on a series of drawings. The design worked on paper, the next step would be to design it using CAD. This was done and the design was found to be both aesthetically pleasing and at the same time very innovative.

Next up were a series of maquettes or scale models. This was my favorite part of the design process since the innovation of the design had been established. The maquettes, although somewhat difficult to assemble, proved the functionality of the design. I began with a cardboard version and worked my way up to a small wooden model held together with a single bolt, as mentioned earlier. The design featured an innovative X-pattern assembly and could be disassembled and re-assembled. This feature allowed the chair to be flat-packed, a very appealing criteria in the furniture design industry.

A scale model or maquette of the hi-back lounge chair, used to determine the viability of the design (2014).

The maquettes encouraged me to continue fleshing out the design. There was a weak link in the rigidity of the design that I would need to address. The attachment of the back of the chair proved to be a challenge since the back was actually a structural component of the chair. It was necessary to build a full-scale version of the chair to better understand this issue. This was accomplished and a focus could be directed to the back of the chair. As a designer, I would always seek a simpler method of creating something.

The original design called for a reinforced panel at the back of the frame. In subsequent designs, it was found that I could easily eliminate this panel by changing some of the design parameters of the lounge chair. The process of developing full-scale models also allowed me to refine the design.

In total, three full-scale mockups of the chair were created. The early versions had a series of lightening holes in the frame to reduce the weight of the chair. Although the holes were somewhat appealing and very contemporary in appearance, I ultimately decided to use solid wood without holes. It was decided that the innovation of the X-pattern frame would be sufficient for this chair. The lightening holes also introduced more steps in making the frame components. Perhaps subsequent versions would incorporate lightening holes. For the sake of the upcoming IDS15 show, it became necessary to finalize a design.

Early prototypes of the new hi- back contemporary styled lounge chair introduced at IDS15. Lightening holes can be seen in the photo (2014).

Once the final design was established, I could begin to develop the processes to create the components. It was an important criterion of the design to make the chair parts repeatable. This involved creating templates for each of the components. The parts could be rough cut using the templates and then dimensioned to final size using hand planes. The joinery used to assemble the chair components was also a challenge. The joints would need to be sufficiently strong to withstand the typical racking forces developed when someone is sitting on a chair. A large part of the design was to work with established chair proportions. The chair would need to have certain measurements that follow ergonomic standards. The depth of the seat and height of the seat both at the front and back were important measurements. It was also decided to make a more contemporary styled hi-back version of the chair for IDS15.

The original design called for a solid surface for both the seat and back. Since the design was also to be marketed as an upscale lounge chair, this would not suffice. Instead, the seat and back were designed to allow for padding and a material covering. The material could be fabric, felt or leather. For IDS15, the two chairs being shown were upholstered in top grain leather. The two chairs were created in both a light wood and dark wood configuration. Although a variety of wood species could be used, the light wood selection was birch whereas the dark wood was walnut. These two species of wood were fairly trendy during this period.

In the weeks leading up to IDS15, I also decided to re-brand "Refined Edge Design". This was something I had wanted to do for a while and kept postponing due to my workload. I decided to incorporate my own last name into a new company name. This would identify me with my designs, add cachet to the brand, and shorten the spelling of the company and domain name. The new company name would now be **Pirollo Design**.

pirollo design

I literally had a few short weeks to accomplish all this and to acquire a new logo as well as promotional items with new branding. With days to spare, I was able to get this all done. The two lounge chairs were upholstered locally and I headed off to IDS15. The show was a success with much interest in the new lounge chair design. As with most large shows, there is much talking and standing. This provided me the opportunity to talk to people about what they like in furniture designs and specifically about my new chair design. The experience was rewarding and I hope to do this again in the future. The chair design has resulted in a few orders since the show.

Today, I continue to develop furniture designs that are contemporary and innovative. Enjoyment is derived in creating furniture designs that are somewhat different than existing, established designs. This has now become the cornerstone of my furniture-making credo. My entry into the art world has also allowed me to cross-pollinate techniques and ideas from one discipline to the other. The woodworking articles authored also allow me to share my knowledge and expertise.

I often look back at the considerable changes in the computer industry over past decades. When compared to woodworking, I continue to market the same jewelry box developed almost twenty years earlier!

Hi-back lounge chair with X-pattern frame entered at IDS15 (2015)
©2015 Marc Lavoie - Courtesy Marc Lavoie Photography.

A few of the labeled promotional items created for the IDS15 show.

Author, Norman Pirollo at a workbench in this recent photo (2015)

Conclusion

"To succeed, you need to find something to hold on to, something to motivate you, something to inspire you"

Tony Dorsett

I HOPE YOU HAVE enjoyed this book and it has motivated and inspired you to move forward with your own journey. The best years of my life have been while self-employed in the creative environment of my woodworking business. I have often told myself that if the business fails, I could easily return to the workforce with a new set of skills. Reciting this has given me peace of mind and failure has thankfully never occurred.

The author maintains a blog of his woodworking, which chronicles furniture created in his studio at:

http://www.refinededge.blogspot.com

http://www.pirollodesign.com/news

As well as offering online woodworking instruction through:

http://www.woodskills.com

About The Author

AS FURNITURE DESIGNER AND AUTHOR, Norman Pirollo has acquired an education from contemporary artisans as well as a breadth of insight into both the visual and decorative arts. Through an equal amount of patience, attention to detail and a keen sense of design, Norman creates striking furniture incorporating unique, contemporary designs. Applying cumulative skills and expertise, he pursues the design process from preliminary sketches to CAD drawing to making.

His work has been featured in books such as "Studio Furniture: Today's Leading Woodworkers", "Wood Art Today 2", "500 Cabinets", "Rooted" as well as "Fine Woodworking", "Woodwork", "Ottawa Life", "Ottawa Citizen", "Panoram Italia", "NICHE Magazine" and other publications. Norman is also an award-winning artist through **www.normanpirollo.com**. He author's woodworking related courses and tutorials through **www.woodskills.com**. The woodworking courses share knowledge and expertise acquired over the years. He currently maintains a contemporary furniture design + build blog at **refinededge.blogspot.com**. Norman resides and operates his furniture design + build studio, **www.pirollodesign.com**, in a country setting in Ottawa, Ontario.

www.ingramcontent.com/pod-product-compliance
Lightning Source LLC
Chambersburg PA
CBHW070656100426
42735CB00039B/2161